Bristol Ra

Hilda Cashmore

Pioneering community worker
and founder of Bristol's Barton Hill Settlement

Helen Meller

ISBN 978-1-911522-62-1

Bristol Radical History Group. 2021.
www.brh.org.uk
brh@brh.org.uk

Contents

The only extant portrait image of Cashmore, taken in 1934.

Introduction

When Hilda Cashmore finally succeeded in creating her first and most important settlement in Bristol in 1911, she had set the course of her life's work. She was to take the idea of a university settlement and transform it.

In terms of the residential university settlement movement in the UK, Bristol University Settlement was the last to be founded in England, just before the First World War, when the movement was still fairly buoyant. It was also the first and only one to have a woman as its first warden, something Hilda Cashmore achieved because she and her friend and supporter, Marian Pease, fought for it. She had wanted to establish a university settlement because she needed a civic institution like Bristol University, neutral in politics and non-religious, to give her venture authority and, above all, because the university had a reputation of being supportive of women. She was actually on the staff of the university as a lecturer in history at the Day Training College for Women, part of the university which she had joined in 1904. The university settlement movement in Britain had been launched in 1884 by the Rev. Samuel Barnett, a Bristol man who had taken a parish in Whitechapel, East End of London. It had an established history that was widely understood, thus potentially securing acceptance for her settlement, not only from the university but from the city of Bristol as well.

She wanted to build on the accepted settlement movement history but radically change its objectives towards meeting the main social challenges of her time. She belonged to a later generation than those who had followed the Rev. Samuel Barnett. The main objective for his settlement, Toynbee Hall, had been to bring young, all male graduates from Oxford to live in the East End of London, in his parish at St Jude's, to see with their own eyes the conditions under which the poor of the East End lived. He was attempting to introduce a new element into the philanthropic world and help renew the philanthropic response to poverty, which was just then, in the early 1880s, becoming once more a social issue and gaining more publicity: about its extent, its social consequences and the need to make the rich understand the problems of the poor.[1]

Cashmore was working a good generation later, after the turn of the century, when even the government had become rattled about the condition of the poor.[2] A major Royal Commission on the Poor Laws argued about the strengths and weaknesses of this penal framework for the provision of social services for four long years between 1905–9. But there was no consensus. Two Reports were published: the majority report opted for the status quo to remain, while the minority report, signed by just four people (under Fabian Socialist influence because Beatrice Webb had been appointed to the Commission), wanted a restructuring of government departments which would then create a state administration for social policies decided at a national level. There was an impasse and the Poor Law stayed. For Cashmore, however, neither the majority nor the minority report was acceptable. She had a wider, more inclusive vision that she demonstrated in all her work for settlements. She believed, along with many of her generation, that what had been achieved in building a democratic, socially just society had been paltry, regardless of the extension of the franchise, which had still not been extended to women.

Cashmore was not convinced that the route being followed by current and even future governments would be ready to tackle the huge, established inequalities in modern society. As cities grew and the economic structure of cities changed, how were people to adjust to living through this broader process of constant change, which bore particularly heavily upon women and children? Some did thrive, but many did not. To help the latter, she wanted an ongoing development of modern social services which should have a strong focus on the individual city, the specific problems citizens faced and how these experiences, when fed into the process of social policy making, might make some difference. Even more important to her, though, was how new ideas of the possibilities of such services were identified. She understood very clearly as a woman, born in 1876, how the issues of class and gender, magnified in the British Empire by race, worked against the liberation of individuals. These contextual issues mitigated against any chance that voices of all citizens would be heard or that the experience of disadvantaged people might have some impact on shaping government social policy.

She did not set out to change the world, she was always very modest about her objectives. But she did believe that she *could* do something, and that she *should* do something, to empower those left behind or damaged by rapid economic and social change. She wanted to explore what it was like at the 'rock face', with hands-on experience and to develop social policies from 'the bottom up'. She did not think that state legislation would solve all the problems without a strong relationship between the state and individual cities across the country. The settlement idea, where social workers would be residents, working and learning about a neighbourhood at first hand, thus had obvious attractions. She envisaged that such a civic institution could both facilitate the implementation of state solutions and offer knowledge and advice, based on practical local experience of particular needs and which social policies worked. Not just the localities, but the whole city was her canvas. She believed that the great cities of the UK, each unique in its history and current economic and social base, were the building blocks of modern society and contained within them both the potential and the challenges of modern life. This for her was the trajectory of the work she wanted to do at a university settlement in a provincial city like Bristol. Her settlement would be based in a particular neighbourhood but would have a city-wide remit.

What follows in the four sections of this book looks at how she developed these ideas in different contexts: in Bristol, her first and most important experiment, and later in Manchester, where she went to save from collapse the first ever provincial university settlement, which had been founded in 1895. In Manchester too, she responded to the city's housing programme, which involved many new housing estates being built around the city. Her concern was for the people who moved into them and the people left behind in central city districts, both groups facing huge challenges in adjusting to social change and their futures. She took the experience she had had in Bristol with community centres on new housing estates, connecting them with settlement city centre services. During part of that period, she was also the leading 'star' of the British settlement movement, becoming the first woman president and also the first from the provinces to lead the organisation representing residential settlements, making a valiant attempt to modernise the British movement. Finally, her last four years of settlement work, from 1934–38, were in India, where she worked in a totally different context, culturally and socially, and in the countryside rather than a big city. A short epilogue offers a brief insight into what happened at Bristol University Settlement post Second World War and to settlements generally in their period of decline in influence and the signs of very modest new growth in the twenty-first century.

Marian Pease, 1912.

University College, Tyndall's Park, 1908.

1. Creating a university settlement in Bristol

Hilda Cashmore: biographical details

Intimate biographical details of Hilda Cashmore and her life are difficult to come by. She was not just extremely reticent herself, but also, unfortunately, few primary sources for her life and work have survived. Personal source material is particularly thin, but at least there are some letters she wrote to others, the most significant being those to Marian Pease. Pease was to quote copiously from these letters in Hilda's Memorial volume, which she lovingly edited.[3] Marian was 84 when Hilda died in 1943, but she managed over the following two years to put together fourteen tributes from Hilda's closest friends, chosen to cover each stage in her life. Marian used information and more quotations from the letters she had received from Hilda about her activities in France and Poland. For her Indian adventure, Marian is the only source. She produced many quotations from Hilda's letters, providing dates and places and occasionally a few sentences to give some context. This is the only extant information on Hilda's work there and the only source of the authentic sound of her voice and her personality.

Marian also wrote an introductory note in the volume that gives the most succinct overview of the basic facts of Hilda's life:

Hilda Cashmore was born on August 22nd, 1876, at Norton Malreward Court, about six miles from Bristol. She was the fifth of a family of six sisters. She was educated at home and at the Ladies' College, Cheltenham. She entered Somerville College, Oxford, in 1899, taking her finals in 1902. [degrees were not given to women] She then taught for two years in the Chesterfield Pupil Teacher Centre, residing at, and taking an active part in the work of the Chesterfield Settlement.

In 1904 she was appointed Tutor and Lecturer in Modern History at the Day Training College, affiliated to University College, Bristol. Then for fifteen years (1911–26) she was Warden of University Settlement, Bristol, and for seven years (1926–33) Warden of the Manchester University Settlement. She was in India from 1934–38, then returned to East Bristol till, at the end of her last illness, she was removed to the British

Hospital for Mothers and Babies, at Woolwich, of which her sister Maud is Matron, where she died on November 15th 1943.

Marian also published a little snippet about Hilda's childhood from her most beloved sister, Maud:

As children we took a great interest in politics. My father was a Liberal and a great Free-Trader. There was a long room over the stables that was often used for political meetings which thrilled us to the marrow, and we used to take the pony-cart and a pot of paste and paste posters over our opponents' posters in the villages around about.

Hilda got a scholarship for Oxford and from then on, all our sympathies were on the Labour side. In the vacations we read much Political Economy and Trade Unionism together.

This makes clear Hilda's political allegiance. But Marian fails to mention that Hilda not only rejected her father's politics, but his Anglican religion as well. It remains unclear when she became a Quaker, though it was possibly at Oxford. This momentous decision materially influenced her thinking about cities, social problems and the nature of poverty—all major Quaker concerns in the early decades of the twentieth century. Equally importantly, the Quakers were to support her strongly in her ventures, especially in India, as they grew to appreciate her outstanding abilities.

Marian does mention *en passant* Hilda's profound love of the countryside, spiritual in its intensity. This passion sustained her when her settlement work in Bristol, and later Manchester, meant she spent much of her adult life living in old, dilapidated inner-city districts. When in Bristol, she managed to go for weekends to Marian Pease's country cottage in the Quantocks, often with Marian or with a party of young people from the settlement. During her time in Bristol, she felt that contact with the countryside was vitally important for everybody's mental and physical health and found ways of enabling groups and families from the settlement neighbourhood to go to the countryside for holidays, something that they had never done before. She shared her love of nature, as well as her commitment to social service, with her favourite sister Maud, the youngest of the family.

Their deep religious faith made them both determined to spend their lives serving people and communities. Maud became a dedicated nurse and midwife and devoted her life to the training of midwives, in which she was very successful. Maud worked in Bristol with Alice Gregory and a widow, Mrs Lelia Parnell, before moving to London where in 1905 the three colleagues established a home for mothers and babies that eventually became the British Hospital for Mothers and Babies, with large new purpose-built premises opened by Queen Mary in 1922.[4] Maud and Hilda kept in close touch and Hilda sent her Bristol students to Maud for training. Hilda herself was a very gifted nurse, a skill that she was to use in many situations in her work. Hilda's character, though, was not like that of her sister. She had an exuberant, outgoing personality and an enormous amount of energy. She was optimistic when she believed in what she was doing and was always able to enthuse people around her. She was also a private person, perceptive at seeing when other people needed help, never seeking it for herself.

She had a wide circle of friends in every walk of life, many of her women friends remaining close over the course of her life. When she thought any of them needed support or simple nursing during periods of personal difficulty, she would quietly provide it, however long it took.[5] When she was in India, a string of young Quaker women, many of them personal friends, were sent out to keep her company on her travels around the Indian sub-continent and at her settlement and ashram in India. She kept in touch with them all through a copious correspondence. It was Marian Pease, however, who played the most important part in Hilda's life, even the crucial one of bringing her to Bristol. The two women had first met in Bristol when Hilda was still a student at Somerville College Oxford. Hilda had been given a letter of introduction to Marian and had visited her, possibly in 1902, to ask her advice about what she should do on graduation. Marian was at the time the Mistress of Method of the Women's Day Training College at Bristol University College, a title more appropriate for someone who trained elementary school teachers. She had been invited to set up this women's college in 1892 but was never given the title of 'director' due to being a woman and teaching women who were not on degree courses.

Marian advised Hilda to get some teacher training. At the same time, she was very impressed by her. For both women some higher education and professional training was critical to their futures. In 1904, when the Women's Day Training College found itself under increasing pressure because of the 1902 Education Act, Marian's department was given a new post for someone who could teach degree courses and she asked Hilda to apply. It was to bring them together and they became close friends. The university settlement project grew out of their many discussions over the next years as the fortunes of the Women's Day Training College continued to wane, and Marian was able to help Hilda with her contacts in Bristol and the social work she had done in the city twenty years before. It was a very fruitful partnership for both. In many ways, Marian Pease (1859–1954) was an exemplary figure in the pioneering generation of women who sought work outside the home, in her case in social work and teaching. She was the second child of her father's third wife. He was a Quaker industrialist whose first and second wives had between them borne him 13 children. His third wife, Susanna Fry, had two children, a boy, Edward, and Marian. Susanna was active in temperance and peace groups and was president of the local branch of what was to become the National Council of Women.

Marian's mother brought her closer to the Fry family and to the network of social workers from the Quaker Meeting House in central Bristol that had been involved in pioneering new kinds of social work in the city for half a century before Hilda arrived.[6] Her brother, Edward Pease, was to make a name for himself in London, joining the Fabian Socialists and becoming Sidney Webb's assistant and secretary of the Fabian Society. He also wrote the first account of the Society.[7] Marian and Hilda, however, were definitely not Fabian Socialists and Marian joined Hilda in her support for Labour. As a young woman, Marian was to achieve a high profile at Bristol University College, being one of the very first women students to study for a degree on its opening in 1876 (the year of Hilda's birth).[8] She was given one of the four temporary two-year scholarships that Catherine Winkworth, a passionate advocate of higher education for women in Bristol, had funded with the help of her friends. Later, on Catherine's death in 1878, the scholarships were made permanent as a memorial to Catherine, helping Marian to finish her degree.[9] Both Marian and Hilda were able to create a strong presence as employees of the University, Marian and her ten years of work with the Day Training College, and Hilda with her teaching and the popularity of her courses amongst the students. Hilda's lectures were open to students across the university who were interested in what she had to say about the economic and social conditions of modern Britain.

Both were committed to introducing social work training at the university as a means of opening up further job prospects for women. There was just one chance card in their hands that really helped their cause. In the preceding years, Bristol University College had been engaged in a campaign to get its charter of independence, and this led to debates amongst students and the local press about the role of the university in the city. A key topic was the possible role of the university in providing training for social workers who might nurture an increase in social services in the city. A wave of new universities was being created since the turn of the century and it was to change perceptions of what a provincial university was meant to be. William Whyte, in his study *Redbrick: a social and architectural history of Britain's civic universities,* quotes the editor of the *Bristol University College Gazette* (May 1908) who posed the question "What is a modern University?" Its answer was very clear: A 'modern university' is a local institution, governed by a mixture of academics and lay people. It is democratic. It provides training in modern disciplines—indeed "Research is the keynote of a modern University". That, for Pease and Cashmore, most definitely included the training of social workers and research in the social sciences.[10]

Getting the project off the ground

In the end, however, the settlement movement did not benefit much as the swathe of new 'red brick' university colleges battled for their independence. Establishing studies in social work and administration was rarely near the top of the agenda in the campaigns. Bristol University College was to be one of six provincial institutions to seek independence between 1900 and the First World War. These were Birmingham in 1900, Manchester and Liverpool in 1903, Leeds in 1904, Sheffield in 1905 and Bristol in 1909. This momentum had to be sustained, most importantly, by private philanthropy, since government funding for these institutions was virtually non-existent. It meant that to raise funds, each university college had to have the publicity and press that drew in the entire city which, on occasion, boosted the idea that the new 'university' should play a role in supporting social services. Some big philanthropists, though, like Joseph Chamberlain in Birmingham, were keener to create a new model for the university with an emphasis on benefitting the economy of the city and its culture.[11] Chamberlain had been impressed by what was happening in American universities, just now finding their feet, having initially looked to European models.[12] He had even managed to get a donation of £50,000 from Andrew Carnegie if he promised to mould Birmingham's development on American lines.

That seemingly did not include an American approach to the development of social services. Birmingham did not create a university settlement, a common occurrence in US universities in big cities. Instead, an arrangement was made with the already existing independent Birmingham Women's Settlement. This meant no overheads for the university and the fees covered the costs of giving Birmingham women students practical training. The Dean of the Faculty of Commerce, Professor WJ Ashley, responsible for integrating this arrangement, saw it as a good opportunity for women.[13] In his view, women were best suited to dealing with office work since "women are peculiarly fitted for much of the administrative work which belongs to local government".[14] It is an insight into the significant gender prejudices Cashmore and Pease were up against in trying to get Bristol to agree to their plan for a university settlement. Whilst women had been in charge of women's settlements, set up by Henrietta Barnett and her friends to counter the maleness of Toynbee Hall, these women's settlements were designed more to continue acceptable female roles in philanthropic work, especially as seen by Octavia Hill and the Charity Organisation Society (COS). Their main function had been to train women in Hill's methods and those of COS, while offering them a pleasant, safe, club-like place to live while gaining practical experience. One example of this was rent collecting as a means of connecting with the poor, ensuring discipline through this function and working to improve the home environment of tenants.

Of the six universities founded in the pre-war wave, only Manchester already had a university settlement, set up in 1895 under the influence of Barnett's suggestion that all provincial cities should have them.[15] The only other newly independent university to acquire a university settlement was Liverpool.[16] This city already had a women's settlement, the Victoria Women's Settlement, which gave women a chance to lead, largely because it was financially supported by William Rathbone whose daughter, Eleanor Rathbone, worked there. She began what was to be a close partnership with the new warden, Elizabeth Macadam, who was appointed in 1903. Macadam had trained in London in Charity Organisation Society methods, an organisation founded in 1869 with

Toynbee Hall, Whitechapel.

Sunday afternoon in the Whitechapel Picture Gallery,
Canon Barnett as guide.

the aim of making charity more efficient and organised and thus able to reach the 'deserving' poor before they had to face the workhouse. Branches of the COS were set up across the country. COS workers, largely women, had also created the first training courses for voluntary social workers, which introduced casework as a 'scientific' method of ascertaining who should and who should not be helped (in terms of their moral characters). Men and women under this aegis would sit on local panels, sifting the 'deserving' from the 'undeserving' amongst the applicants for relief.

When Liverpool University got its charter, the two women wanted to go further, concentrating on the relationship between the state and the voluntary sector in social services.[17] Since William Rathbone was an important donor, they tended to get their way. But events were to overwhelm their intentions. Young people, especially in northern and midland cities, had become angry for some years at philanthropic responses to poverty. In Bradford, in 1904, a group had set up what they called 'The Guild of Help', a voluntary organisation that rejected COS strictures on how to deliver relief and with it the social science training organised by the COS.[18] Within a few years, there were 60 Guilds in towns and cities across the country, with a total membership of 8000.[19] This far outnumbered those in the Charity Organisation Societies and their support. The new Liverpool University Settlement had to scramble to get itself set up as a branch of the Guild of Help so as to engage the interest of students in undertaking social studies.

However, the newly appointed Warden of Liverpool University Settlement, a clergyman (it had to be a man), Frederick D'Aeth, made his first initiative the tracking down and listing of charitable organisations in the whole Liverpool region.[20] His work had echoes of the COS model in that the objective was to find a way to co-ordinate existing charitable effort as a coherent whole through agreed bureaucratic structures. It had no dynamic relating to social change. But his work was ultimately instrumental in the creation, in 1909, of Liverpool Charity and Voluntary Services, a huge charitable organisation run on business lines, maximizing efficiencies of scale and aiming at sharing resources across the region. His efforts were recognised, giving a boost to the city's voluntary sector.[21] In a city as large as Liverpool, with massive social problems, this initiative gradually transformed over the decades, resulting in a private company with a budget of millions, consisting of earnings from delivering paid-for services, and major grants from the government and philanthropic trusts. It had developed a remit to cover a huge range of services, some similar, some supplementary, to those being created by the state.

In Bristol, the context for the challenge facing Cashmore and Pease in founding their settlement was very different. They had to find a way of getting the university to accept the idea of a university settlement without sacrificing their independence, so they could pursue their own ideas and objectives. This was central to any success since their ideas were unconventional. They had no intention of creating a women's settlement. But negotiating with the University was not easy, either getting acceptance of the idea of a university settlement or getting terms and conditions that would safeguard their much-desired independence. Marian Pease had already witnessed the full gamut of what university support could mean for an ancillary institution from her time working for the Women's Day Training College. It had gone from enthusiasm for training women teachers when there was a fat grant to be earned, to letting the support slide when men were being promoted by government legislation and the training of male teachers got even fatter grants.

In the years after Hilda joined the Women's Day Training College, Pease found ever more difficulties in keeping it going. One of her problems was her own lack of status when the changes occurred after the Education Act of 1902.[22] She may have achieved a higher profile than any other female member of staff at the whole university college through her work at the Women's Day Training College but had not been given the title "Director" and did not have the salary grades and conditions of other academic staff.[23] It was to lead to many difficulties that indirectly impinged on plans for the settlement. Bristol University College was very keen to benefit from the bigger grants and quickly established a Men's Day Training College and a Training College for Secondary Education Teaching. But the men's college was not brought together amicably with the women's college. The man appointed as its director, Thomas Sutcliffe Foster, was immediately put in charge of all three units. The result was an administrative muddle that was to downgrade the original women's college in every respect. Student grants for men were double those for women and they were given better hostels with more space, domestic facilities and even better food! As for Pease, her own position was profoundly affected. Unfortunately, Foster was neither good at administration nor very willing to cooperate with established staff. The complications of the arrangements led to great disagreements and distress, not only for the women but also for the university administrators who had to sort them out.[24]

As for the women students, they went from being the largest group of women students across the whole university, there being very few women in other disciplines, to being reduced in number as the men's college was established. It was the end of a pioneering era.[25] The male teacher training students had better job prospects. They could apply for and take jobs in both elementary and secondary schools since secondary education for boys was now being developed. Men had the attraction for future employers that they were career-orientated whilst women teachers had to quit their jobs if they married because of the marriage bar. The numbers of Pease's students, formerly many drawn from the pupil-teacher system in the now defunct Board Schools, began to dry up. Pease was an excellent teacher, and she did her best to encourage young women from local schools to continue to apply for courses and qualify.[26] She put up twelve students in her own large home at Westbury-on-Trym to minimise their costs. In 1904 she managed to get an extra post to improve the range of subjects offered to women students and teach them to a higher standard. That had led to the appointment of Hilda Cashmore to lecture on modern history, so introducing courses that could lead to degree status and thus teaching posts in secondary education.

From the earliest days, Pease and Cashmore had been discussing the urgent need to find new options for training women for other kinds of professional work beyond teaching as one of the main objectives of the settlement. Top of the list was social work of all kinds. They needed to be independent to do this, but at the same time, they wanted the university to give status to their settlement and to endorse the social work courses they did in a proper manner, enhancing their reputation. Cashmore had started a groundswell of demand for a settlement in the only way open to her, by inspiring those she came into contact with, her students. She gave lectures on economic and social history and the value of social work and encouraged students to join the Guild of Voluntary Social Service that she set up. Her approach was very popular, and she began recruiting large numbers to the Guild—for example in just one year, she recruited 120 out of the total of 150 students that formed the cohort of students across the whole university college and day training college. They were flocking to join the Guild and their enthusiasm spread amongst the student body.

Professor Conwy Lloyd Morgan.   George Hare Leonard.

She may have got the support of Bristol's students for a university settlement, but the university establishment was not necessarily to be swayed by the same idealism. However, some key individuals came to the rescue. One of these was Conwy Lloyd-Morgan, out-going President of the University College, who in his youth, as a contemporary of Patrick Geddes, the pioneering sociologist and future town planner, had become interested in the latter's ideas, especially about the need for more social science research on modern cities. Others included George Hare Leonard, the HO Wills Professor in Modern History since 1905, who had been warden of the Broad Plain Settlement, an educational settlement known as the 'Poor Man's University', and Arthur Skemp, Winterstoke Professor of English, who had just arrived at Bristol from Manchester, where he had been a pillar of Manchester University Settlement. They were few but influential. Professor Lloyd-Morgan had witnessed the treatment meted out to the Women's Day Training College. He recognised the need to help women students now get jobs in social work and was willing to throw his weight vigorously behind the project.

He knew from experience the competence of Pease and Cashmore and was very happy to support the latter as warden of the settlement. He later became the first President of the Settlement Council. He also chaired the first of two important meetings called in 1910 to decide the fate of the settlement project. The first meeting, a closed one for university staff only, was to convince them that the settlement idea was a good thing for the university. The invited speaker was John Kelman, theologian and member of the Edinburgh University Settlement, there being strong support for settlement work in Scotland.[27] He claimed that a settlement made a university complete as an educational force for all classes, while offering practical experience for students of the social sciences. Hostile opinion in the university began to shift a little.

The second meeting was open and public, to encourage support from the city, civic bodies and local philanthropists. The chairman was Bristol's Lord Mayor. Many representatives from organisations in the city came, including trade unions and the Women's Co-operative Guild, but also large numbers of students turned up to show their support by sheer numbers.[28] The hall was so crowded that students were sitting on windowsills and standing in the aisles. The invited speaker was Sir Oliver Lodge, Vice-Chancellor of Birmingham University, who happened also to be the brother of Professor Richard Lodge, a key figure in the Edinburgh Settlement. Lodge drew on the experience of success in Birmingham as the university had worked in partnership with the established women's settlement to offer training in practical social work in the city, of benefit both to students and citizens. Lodge finished on a high moral note with a heartfelt appeal for "sacrifice and work to bring the kingdom of Heaven on earth", the clarion call of 'social citizenship'. This clinched it and the meeting erupted in thunderous applause. The university's new Vice-Chancellor, Sir Isambard Owen, had attended the meeting and made supportive, if rather indistinct, noises. But he knew now that he would have to go along with the settlement plan.

Isambard Owen.

As for Pease and Cashmore, they managed to get what they wanted: academic support from the university whilst keeping their independence.[29] The price they had to pay was financial; there was very little university funding, so they had to be constantly alert to the need to raise funds to keep going. Ever the optimist, Cashmore was not at all fazed by that and she was proved right. The settlement survived for many decades, bumping along with a small deficit. The great thing was that now they could actually start on making a reality of all their plans. There followed two years of exceptional work, dealing with all the immediate challenges. The earliest steps were to decide on a location for the settlement and start to raise funds to get it up and running. Pease and Cashmore were at least prepared for this. A key figure helping them was a good friend of Marian Pease, Mabel Tothill, with whom she had worked way back in the 1880s and early 1890s, when she had devoted herself to voluntary work for girls.[30] Mabel Tothill had been a fellow helper with Marian in a project to set up a girls' club in Barton Hill, an early example in the city of the recognition that in terms of charitable effort for young people, girls and their welfare were almost totally ignored. It made sense when looking for a site for the settlement to choose Barton Hill, where both Pease and Tothill had local knowledge and contacts.[31]

Tothill was also to help magnificently with raising the money for the settlement. Tothill and her sister had recently lost both their parents and together had inherited the family wealth.[32] Mabel was to make the first big donation, which paid for the purchase of the cottages in Barton Hill that could be transformed into the settlement. Tothill, like Cashmore, had converted to Quakerism and these three friends, Pease, Tothill and Cashmore, formed a formidable trio in the cause: Pease with her leadership and administrative experience, Tothill with her personal commitment and her wealth, and Cashmore with her enthusiasm, intelligence and ability to organise and inspire. It was to be called the Bristol University Settlement but direct university support for the immediate challenges was fairly thin, some financial support towards purchasing the properties and some maintenance costs once the settlement was established. More university help came from individuals amongst the university staff, some personal donations and invaluable support from a few who took up positions on the Settlement Council. Further financial assistance came from the fact that Pease, Cashmore and their new young colleague, Lettice Jowitt, still all worked at the Women's Day Training College and continued on salaries commensurate with the hours they worked as lecturers and tutors, Cashmore working the fewest hours as her warden role increased.

The cottages that became the University Settlement.

Support was to grow between the settlement and Bristol's city council but again not with promises of funding. Early actions were the unofficial, personal ones of individuals, a key one of which came from the wealthy industrialist, Stanley Badock (1867–1945), who was Bristol's Sheriff in 1908–9. He was also a strong supporter of the university and became a long-standing member of the University Council, taking leading positions on its executive over many years. In his year of office as Sheriff, he had made his major philanthropic objective the founding of the Bristol Civic League of Social Service, connecting organised voluntary and public social work in the city. This was chaired by the wife of the then Mayor, the industrialist Edward Robinson. Mrs Robinson had overseen the creation of the Bristol Social Service League, made up of the Bristol Charity Organisation Society, together with other charities for poor relief, but also the Juvenile Recreation Committee and other new social projects of the city Council. The COS and other charities organising poor relief were definitely not to be within the settlement remit. However, Badock was ready to support them all, including the new settlement when it was formed.[33]

Badock recommended the architect, Sir George Oatley, who had modernised his own home, Holmwood House, in 1905, to help transform the Barton Hill cottages into a residential settlement. Within the structures of three of the cottages, Oakley discovered the remains of an eighteenth-century farmhouse and did an excellent job in opening this up to create a coherent, pleasant and functional set of buildings with accommodation for twelve residents, meeting rooms and a courtyard and garden. Some ancillary cottages were bought up to provide extra residential accommodation. Elizabeth Sturge, who had had a great deal of experience with her own projects of building working-class housing, volunteered to act as the unpaid project manager on site.[34] When the settlement was up and running, Stanley Badock's mother also made a significant contribution by recruiting volunteers. She had been a leading force in the foundation of Badminton School, a boarding school for girls. She encouraged the school to become a strong supporter of the settlement, and for years, numbers of girls volunteered to work there.[35]

Best of all though, in Cashmore's view, was the support from trade unions, friendly societies and co-operative societies, together with small, even very small, donations from many Bristolians, regardless of personal wealth and influence. This was just the type of welcome and personal support that Cashmore really wanted, though larger gifts were also urgently required. A steady list of regular subscribers was needed but this did cause some problems as she was not prepared for subscribers to dictate any actions at the settlement simply on the grounds that they were paying large subscriptions. She was quite ready to strike off the list anyone who tried to interfere. Quite early on a female member of the Wills family wrote to say that she did not think it was appropriate that Mabel Tothill should be a resident at the settlement. She did not name her directly, just complained that she was not in favour of supporters of women's suffrage. We do not know whether she was aware that Mabel was not just a passionate supporter of women's suffrage, but also a socialist, heavily involved with the East Bristol Labour party and a strong supporter of pacifism. Needless to say, Cashmore reacted very firmly indeed to this. She wrote back: "I can imagine no lady of any age or experience, living in a university settlement, who would care to be dictated to".[36] There is no evidence of what happened next and whether Elizabeth Wills withdrew her subscription, but much to Hilda's personal dismay, Mabel decided to relinquish her position as a resident of the settlement. However, she still kept closely in touch with what was going on in Barton Hill and continued to donate generously to projects such as the Outdoor School for Sick Children. Professor Conwy Lloyd-Morgan, now the President of the Settlement Council, and other Council members, warmly supported Cashmore in this affair. Cashmore could not publicly reveal her own sympathies, but they were obvious to those who worked with her at the Settlement. She showed her support for causes by her actions: for the peace movement, going to France with the Quakers in the First World War to help civilian victims; and for her political stance, by lecturing to trade unions by invitation and working closely with the Women's Co-operative Society and Labour trade unionists such as Ernest Bevin[37].

To supplement subscriptions, she managed to earn a respectable income for the settlement by developing fee-paying courses of social service training. With links made through the Women's Day Training College and Marian Pease's strong support, Cashmore was able to set up a social services diploma—known as the Testamur—with the university acting as the validating body. This gave the qualification a national standing that made it possible for her to attract students from further afield than Bristol. It also tied the University to the settlement in an academic role, thus justifying its name as a university settlement. But there still was not enough money in the first two years to pay the warden a salary. Cashmore worked anyway, without pay, and after two years she made that permanent, though she was paid for some part-time history lectures at the university.[38] However, the university did provide an essential element for the survival of the settlement by continuing to offer accreditation to supplementary courses set up and run by the settlement in the field of social work and allowing the settlement to be paid the fees directly.[39] It had academic independence with courses designed by the lecturers themselves, initially all from the Day Training College: Cashmore herself, Marian Pease, and a new young colleague, Lettice Jowitt.[40]

Cashmore's equally strong desire for the settlement to be seen as independent within the settlement movement as a whole was more difficult to demonstrate, depending as it did on publicity and personal contacts. Pease and Cashmore wanted to flag up their different viewpoint from the settlement movement of Barnett and Toynbee Hall, from women's settlements, and even from other university settlements. They were not at all hostile to Toynbee Hall or these other settlements. The problem was one of publicity-getting their message and their objectives

Rev. S. A. and Mrs Barnett at the time of their marriage in 1873.

across to the people of Bristol. The biggest public difficulty was on their own 'doorstep'. The Rev. Samuel Barnett was a Bristol man and had a house in Clifton where he and his wife Henrietta stayed every year. It helped them stay in touch with his brother, still resident in Bristol, and their many personal friends in the city.[41] His work founding the residential university settlement movement had given him a national and international reputation. But he was to find that the Anglican hierarchy, especially in London where he had his parish, were not impressed by the fact that he seemed to prioritize social issues over the religious, singularly failing to fill his parish church on Sundays. But since the Anglican Church is the established church of the country, recognition of his work could come from parliament. Lord Herschell, the Lord Chancellor of the day, in charge of Anglican preferments, decided that, because of Barnett's connections with Bristol, he should be awarded a canonry at the Cathedral there in 1893.[42]

Barnett was delighted and was known henceforth as Canon Barnett. He had no intention of living full-time in Bristol, so he wrote a little pamphlet for Bristol citizens as his 'return' gift for his elevation. Its title was *The Ideal City*. It was basically a Liberal manifesto that he had written ten years earlier in 1883, some months before the opening of Toynbee Hall.[43] His words were for the philanthropic male elite in the city, mostly of a Liberal persuasion, suggesting they could make Bristol an 'Ideal City' if they funded all kinds of modern civic facilities. It was their moral duty to show 'social citizenship'.[44] But by 1911, Barnett's version of 'social citizenship' had been strongly challenged by trade unionists and labour activists who were to see it as an insult: 'civic philanthropy' in lieu of better wages and working conditions.[45] Cashmore needed to distance herself from this clash since it had very little to do with her intentions to make the settlement an independent institution serving all citizens and depending on their voluntary support to do so.

Models for the future: the Quaker manifesto and settlements in North America

Cashmore sought and chose a different inspiration, one that she herself had been influenced by, the recent social endeavours of the Society of Friends. JW Rowntree had made a passionate speech at the 1895 National Annual Quaker Meeting held for the first time in Manchester, imploring the Quakers to turn from their perennial religious disputes and instead unite to invest in and build a new social infrastructure for the citizens of modern Britain.[46] That year, Hilda Cashmore was just nineteen and possibly fairly new in her membership of the Society of Friends. There is no evidence to determine when she left Anglicanism and became a Quaker but JW Rowntree's message calling for Friends to adopt a tolerant yet spiritual faith and to come together to work for a better future society strongly appealed to her. Rowntree was the mouthpiece of the liberal Quakers, the title of his address being "Has Quakerism a Message to the World Today?" An answer was to come from Rufus Jones, a leading member of the American Quakers and credited subsequently as the most important influence on Quakerism in the twentieth century. He said that "Quakers have always been intensely humanitarian". Rufus Jones and JW Rowntree met in 1897 and forged a major friendship, crossing the Atlantic twice a year for major discussions that influenced them both and the Quaker movement.

Hilda Cashmore took Rowntree's question and the answer very seriously and it was to shape her work in all the settlements she created or ran: in Bristol; in Manchester in the mid-years of her life; and her last settlement work in India, in Rasulia and Jamai when she was in her 60s. A critical challenge for JW Rowntree and the liberal Quakers was to gain support from the Quaker sceptics, to convince them that they were simply building on the past history of their sect. Rowntree set up a book series, the Rowntree History Series, exploring the history of the sect and its record in social work. The series ran from 1909–1921, with editors and contributors presenting a nuanced 'history' as a way of demonstrating the relevance and modernity of the Quaker message.[47] It was virtually propaganda and the views the volumes expounded were fiercely contested by many Friends. But it succeeded in creating a narrative of the past that supported the idea that the Quakers had a message for the modern world. It was warmly supported by the liberal Quaker group who happened to include the industrialists and chocolatiers, the Rowntrees in York, the Cadburys in Birmingham and the Frys in Bristol. Members of these families were not only leaders of philanthropy and voluntary social work in their respective cities, but they also made a national impact with the causes they supported.

For them, the period 1895–1925 was the 'golden years' when they made great fortunes, rebuilt their factories, ran them using modern techniques, and could choose the causes they wished to support. The Rowntrees invested especially in adult education, the scientific study of society and workers' housing. The Cadburys built the modern village of Bournville, a prototype of a 'Garden City', became leading protagonists in the national campaign for town planning and endowed many cultural and educational institutions in Birmingham. The Frys in Bristol were slightly less flamboyant and ambitious. They helped to fund the university, develop adult education in the city and provide other leisure facilities as local town councillors and, in the case of Lewis Fry, as a Liberal MP. All these activities gave Hilda a glimpse of a modern future, a direction in which social changes might evolve. But she could not, and did not want to, emulate their projects, which required personal fortunes, male leadership and retained a class dimension whatever the good intentions. What could women with few resources achieve who were not heads of prosperous companies or wives of directors? Or who rejected class or race-based approaches to social and voluntary work? Cashmore was a humanist and wanted to base her work on people, willing to start pragmatically in her city on a modest scale. She did not need huge financial resources to build on the tradition of voluntary social work of Bristol Quakers because, over the past half century or so, they had been becoming more 'humanitarian' than religious already.

The focus of Quaker social work in the city throughout the nineteenth century had been the Quaker Mission in the city centre. Initially a religious mission, in the 1860s the Quakers did something remarkable. A deeply spiritual, serious-minded sect, they yet decided to be the first in the city to take part in new developments in socio-religious work that went against their culture. They transformed their city mission into a community centre, ceasing to mainstream attempts to convert the populace. The Quakers owned a building in New Street, St. Jude's, that had been used to support indigent Quaker weavers in 1696. In 1865 they made it into a meeting place for local people where they could come not only for friendship, advice, comfort and support, but also free entertainment, as a means of attracting them to come. The idea was to connect with the people and to befriend them. Young Quakers began offering entertainments of music, songs, readings and poetry which they performed themselves. Regular Penny Readings on Wednesday evenings were organised, joining the Penny Readings movement that was spreading quickly across the country.[48] There were social activities for mothers and children and adult education for men. The most unusual aspect of their endeavours was that they did this not in any 'respectable' suburb but in the city centre amongst the poorest citizens. Quaker women played a large part in sustaining this initiative. Amongst them were the then young Sturge sisters, all six of them, including Elizabeth Sturge who, as has been noted, was to volunteer help decades later to the University Settlement.

JS Fry (1826–1913) taught Sunday classes and offered adult education since, as a member of the older generation, he preferred this to the more frivolous pursuits.[49] His commitment to adult education had begun early in 1853 at the Bristol branch of the Young Men's Christian Association (he became President in 1877). He taught classes at the Quaker Mission and eventually became the Secretary of the Bristol Adult Education School Association from 1874–1898. All this voluntary effort and enthusiasm kept the Mission thriving for almost three decades. By the 1890s, however, these methods no longer attracted a response from local people. There had been a considerable growth of commercial entertainment and a greater variety of leisure activities was now available. Bristol, for example, had more brass bands than much larger cities in the north; there were huge new music-halls; mushrooming interest in sport, including the establishment of a separate Bristol football league on the Downs; many cycling clubs; and many clubs devoted to various hobbies. Bristol's pubs had diversified, adapting to these changes. It was a very different cultural world which had become important.[50] The strength of this competition meant that by 1895 Quakers had to accept that their modest activities at the Mission (apart from adult education) had lost momentum and were no longer working as a means of connecting with the people. They closed the Mission.

JS Fry continued with his adult education work but faced more hostility from his students, some of whom were workers in his own factory. Fry, belonging to an older generation than the current directors of the Cadbury and Rowntree factories, was perfectly happy to devote his time and energies to helping his workers acquire some adult education but he forbade them to form a trade union.[51] Thus while the actions of the chocolatiers, Frys, Rowntrees and Cadburys, were progressive within the Society of Friends, their enlightened ideas and voluntary social work did have serious limitations. Their progressive approach certainly did not extend to the black workers on their overseas estates.[52] In fact, it was in their own interest as business leaders to consider the uncertainties of the future, both for themselves and their workers: the economic and social challenges and the changing political landscape of Britain.[53] In 1901, however, one of the more academic minded of them, BS Rowntree (unburdened at the time with having to run the firm), was to make a major contribution to social work and social services, publishing his research as a liberal Quaker. His path-breaking social survey, *Poverty: a study of town life*, opened up new possibilities of extending understanding of the causes of poverty, research that was vitally important to politicians, trade unionists and all concerned with social work and policy.[54]

Rowntree was building on the work of Charles Booth who had done the very first social survey in the UK, presenting information on the extent of urban poverty in map form as well as text, Booth's most famous volume being a social survey of poverty in the East End of London (1889).[55] For contemporaries, it was breath-taking.[56] One weakness of Booth's map, however, was that it gave just a static snapshot of the incidence of poverty at one particular moment, since colouring of the map in 1889 to reflect levels of poverty did not allow for any movement. Another was his poverty line, determining levels of poverty, somewhat a matter of guesswork, since defining such a line is extremely difficult. But Booth remained confident that 25% of the population were living in poverty in the light of supporting research based on the 1881 census and the information from school attendance officers and from an army of social investigators, including Beatrice Potter (later Webb), who knocked on doors. However, it was argued at the time that London was not representative of the whole country and that the level of dire poverty might be greater there than elsewhere.

Rowntree's work covered all these issues and more. Adopting a newly sophisticated scientific and statistical approach, he determined a poverty line dependent on the cost of the number of calories needed to maintain the physical efficiency of wage earners. It was somewhat absurd, being very basic and not allowing for choice of foods, only for the cheapest foodstuffs, where prices could still be variable. But at least it was seen as 'scientific'. Much more importantly he was able to establish that for most individuals, the experience of poverty was not a constant. He could relate his data on levels of poverty to a moving pattern of family structures and the life stages of individuals. He was able to do this as his canvas was York, using his family connections to collect data from industrialists as well as labour organisations, and statistical studies had advanced enough for him to use sampling techniques of the population as a whole that could be considered accurate. He was also helped by the fact that York was a modest size, just 75,812 in 1899 when he began his research.[57]

His most remarkable finding was what he called the 'poverty cycle'. His results showed that poverty had a 'dynamic' during the lifetime of individuals and families. He identified three critical periods of poverty for working-class families: childhood, the middle years with dependent family, and finally old age. It introduced the idea that a very high proportion of the urban working classes were in poverty at various stages of their lives, which meant that far more than 25% had direct personal experience of extreme poverty, possibly a majority. Such an understanding lit up new visions for effective voluntary social work. It demanded a rethink too on state welfare policies such as feeding schoolchildren, better health care of workers, but also improved maternity care, enhanced old age pensions and, of course, adjusting the universal approach of the Poor Law itself. Rowntree was also able to collect and highlight critical factors such as the provision of affordable housing and educational facilities at all levels for boys, girls, men and women to help them acquire the necessary skills for new commercial and industrial work.

This work was vital to Hilda Cashmore and her settlement work as she could focus her attention on activities that were in tune with an understanding of the 'poverty cycle'. She could not address poverty, that had to be the work of the state. But the voluntary sector could respond to a wide variety of things that could improve the quality of people's lives, sometimes even just by giving a helping hand in a minor crisis. How to do this was the question. Cashmore, ever practical, knew that she could not, and anyway, did not want to operate like a Quaker industrialist. She was more particularly interested in studying other examples of settlements, run by women, in other countries, especially the USA and Canada, seeing for herself the most up-to-date techniques they were using and the most successful initiatives. After the first hectic months of 1911 were over at the Bristol Settlement, she applied for study leave to the Council of the Day Training College at the university and was granted a two-month sabbatical to study settlements elsewhere. It was to change her life. She pointedly did not go to London, ignoring Toynbee Hall, nor did she go to any of the women's university settlements in London, Liverpool or Birmingham. She went, instead, to university settlements in the USA and Canada, where the settlement movement was currently most thriving, much of it led by women and not gender restricted as in the UK.[58]

There is little evidence of what she found in Canada; Pease only quotes from the letters she received from Cashmore while in the US.[59] There she went to Boston, New York and Chicago. She was overwhelmed by what she found and the intensity of meetings and discussions that she took part in. In Boston she stayed at Denison House and was introduced to so many people, attended so many lectures and had so many meals at the homes of hospitable dons, that she wrote to Pease: "I shall be driven to eschew philanthropy or take it in smaller doses … I shall be driven to the alcoholic habit or turn to tramp". In New York she stayed at the Columbia University Settlement and was taken to Ellis Island where she met with the secretary of the Immigrant Aid Society and saw the horrors that met rural immigrants from all over the world, struggling to find their feet in the city. She was profoundly moved by the scale of the problems of these overseas immigrants. It was, most likely, the inspiration of her later determination to undertake war work with civilian refugees displaced by the First World War. It also made her sensitive to the fact that within twentieth century society, migration, particularly rural to urban migration and its attendant traumas, was not just a common experience in European and especially British cities, but a world-wide phenomenon, especially in her lifetime, within the British Empire.

But it was in Chicago, staying at the North-Western University Settlement where she was longest, that she really engaged with the issues on how to run a settlement and what kind of new ideas were developing around this work. She visited Jane Addams at Hull House several times. What impressed her was the way Addams had managed to develop a social inclusiveness and 'collective efficiency': all classes, races and local institutions cooperating to deal with the often-overwhelming problems of the neighbourhood. The settlement was a contact centre, not just for social workers but for everyone.[60] Volunteers and professionals (a growing number now) worked together, dealing with issues professionally and collaboratively. However, it is also highly likely she met in Chicago the up-and-coming writer on modern states, societies and social work, the Quaker philanthropist, Mary Parker Follett (1868–1933), whose ideas became one of the most important intellectual influences on her future outlook.[61]

Follett, in 1911, was chair of a new initiative, The Women's Municipal League's Committee on Extended Use of School Buildings, a clumsy title but the beginnings of a positive way of creating communities in new neighbourhoods without the cost of buildings, encouraging creative, communal experiences and offering adult education. Follett was to argue that 'Creative Experience' (the title of a book she wrote in 1924) was the essential ingredient of social democracy. She went on to make a stand against modern 'scientific management' in industry (Taylorism), arguing that ignoring human relations and their interaction in the workplace stifled creative thinking and new ideas in industrial development. Cashmore became deeply interested in Follett's ideas, often quoting from her work in her own lectures back in Britain. Her final experience in Chicago concerned a strike. Cashmore witnessed how the North-Western University Settlement workers supported women workers in a garment factory who were striking for shorter working hours: they wanted a 10-hour day. She witnessed their suffering and the fact that they lost. All these experiences gave Cashmore a very modern perspective on twentieth-century social changes and their challenges, dealing with industrial strife, social dislocation, immigration and civic identities.

When Cashmore got back to Bristol from America, she wanted to try out the actions she had witnessed and test whether she could begin to change public assumptions of the purpose and nature of the voluntary work of settlements. But first she had to gain the trust of the ordinary citizens of Bristol who were mostly unfamiliar with the settlement idea and growing more hostile to the kind of social philanthropy that might demand an attitude of deference. Cashmore would not be able to give what she wanted to the city and its citizens without eliminating general ignorance, fears and hostility, and gaining cooperation and active support from those she came into contact with.

2. Bristol University Settlement: a new kind of civic institution

Early activities in the Settlement

Hilda Cashmore started by giving lectures to schools, trade unions and the Women's Co-operative Guild and writing pamphlets explaining her particular approach. Jenny Harrow suggests that when she published *A Catechism on the University Settlement Bristol*, which attempts to give short answers to questions frequently asked,[62] she may have borrowed the format from an American paper written by the famous Chicago settlement worker, Mary Kingsley Simkovitch.[63] Cashmore's pamphlet has subsequently been lost, as has the text of the address she made to school leavers in 1913: *The underlying motive for social work*. Even without the actual evidence of these papers, it is clear that she was not closely following historical assumptions about the settlement movement in the UK. If her ideas needed a British context, she was in tune with the broader movements in social thought in Britain in the early twentieth century that were 'idealist' in character. Idealist thought was extremely varied.

The perspective closest to the one that Cashmore adopted could be found in the work of EJ Urwick, a former sub-warden of Toynbee Hall, who had become the first Director of Social Science and Social Administration at the London School of Economics in 1910.[64] His major work, *A Philosophy of Social Progress* (1912), was firmly based on the idea that, in the complicated context of urban life, new developments had to come from practical work and personal experience. There was no substitute for an 'organic' approach to social work, since people and communities were subject to constant change, from the economic and social context surrounding them as well as their own personal circumstances. He railed against everyone who started from 'paper' plans that seemed like good ideas at the time:

> the individual faddists to sober county councils and even governments, preparing all kinds of schemes of wholesale improvement in the firm belief that they will work. But they never work.[65]

Cashmore might not have been as pessimistic as Urwick but she sympathised with his belief that dealing with social issues needed experience of working with people, though she also thought 'scientific' theories of social science were important. In the last surviving paper from her days as Warden of Bristol University Settlement (which will be discussed in more detail later), she wrote that "the personality of each Settlement is a living growing life (or a decaying one)", a nod to her belief that current social evolutionary theory was the essential ingredient for keeping the project alive. But Cashmore would have been totally with Urwick when he suggested that the underlying motive of voluntary social work was entirely a moral one. Without referring to any religious faith, he yet suggested that "no aim is true which is not spiritual—that is, which is not consciously directed to bringing nearer the attainment of the only absolute good end, the realization of the true individual as supreme over both society and self". He called this the 'social good'.[66]

How to put this all into practice, however, was another thing. When Pease was asked why Barton Hill should be the location of the Bristol settlement, she often replied "It was just a place where some of our friends live", referring to her work there in the 1880s. But obviously a definition of how this could be a method of operating within a particular neighbourhood depended on the cultural context of the moment. Barnett, for instance, had always used the idea of 'friendship' as the central plank of the settlement movement, but he and his wife had tried it when they first arrived at St Jude's vicarage in Whitechapel, at a period when the middle classes were expected to set an example by adhering to the accepted class relations. How that differed totally from the kind of 'friendship' envisaged by the two Bristol Quakers (who also naturally had a very different understanding of the term 'Friends') is demonstrated in Henrietta Barnett's discussion of their first 'party'.

The Barnetts were pioneers in trying this in the East End. Mrs Barnett's party for parishioners, held in the salubrious setting of St. Jude's vicarage in 1872, was envisaged as a cross-class event with everyone behaving in a 'civilised' manner. She recounts that

the people behaved badly. They pushed and scrambled, pocketed the viands, picked the flowers, stole the fruit, made unseemly noises, and rudely frolicked. They also brought people who were not invited, told glib lies as they invented impromptu relations and unexpected lodgers, and smuggled their children in.[67]

Her disdain for this behaviour is palpable. The Barnetts stuck to their idea of teaching what they considered was 'civilised' behaviour as defined by the middle classes. In her biography of her husband, Mrs Barnett devotes a whole chapter to the social events they were eventually able to hold, after years of making their position clear, with totally deferential parishioners who nevertheless (but only according to Mrs Barnett) seemed to have got great pleasure out of these occasions.[68]

For Pease and Cashmore, this way of making friends was both irrelevant and completely alien to them. Working forty years later, they were able to adopt ways of making friends openly, in the totally non-judgmental fashion that they believed in. Through daily practice and sensitive concern, Cashmore personally did make many friends. She had taken up residence in a terraced house along the road from the settlement buildings in case her neighbours would see her as one of 'them' if she lived at the settlement. There are many anecdotes given in her memorial volume of her acts of neighbourliness on an individual basis and in the community at large, from those who were sensitive to her desire to be taken as a friend of her neighbours. Winifred Gill who had been with her in Bristol gave a later example, from her time at the University Settlement in Manchester while again living in a terraced house. She wrote that:

[the] little front room in Every Street in Ancoats, often housed a chance visitor for the night. There was, for instance, the tall, gently spoken woman, her wits just the least little bit out of focus, who sometimes preferred two chairs in Hilda's front room, to the casual ward. "You see, my dear, I can leave you whenever I wish. The arrangements are not quite the same in the other place".[69]

The testimony of her memorial volume shows how she gave and received friendship in abundance from friends, from neighbours and from all who sought her help. They were individual friendships based on trust.

She had a chance to develop that trust on a neighbourhood level in 1912, when she was finding her way as the new warden. Following her experiences in Chicago, she was to witness another great strike, this time in Barton Hill, affecting the women workers of the Great Western Cotton Factory. The whole neighbourhood was caught up in this because the factory was the largest employer of women in the area.

The Great Western Cotton Works in Barton Hill.

Women workers at the Great Western Cotton Works.

There had been earlier strikes, especially a large one in 1889 when the women had been unionised.[70] But this time everything was worse than it had ever been. The factory had been making losses over a number of years and the wages of the women had been cut. This policy had been followed as a possibly misguided effort to keep the factory open, in the awareness that it was a major economic support of the women and their families in the neighbourhood and the hope that trade might pick up again. The women were now without union support as they could not pay the union membership and wages had fallen to just 8 shillings a week in many cases, despite long hours of work.[71]

For the settlement, this was a test in their own back yard, which had the widest consequences for its future. Cashmore had to prove that she and her workers were no middle-class lackeys on the side of the directors of the company (even though Marian Pease's father had been one of them). From the start, Cashmore had made plain that the settlement was not some group of 'do-gooding' middle class philanthropists. Unlike Canon Barnett at Toynbee Hall in the Great Dock Strike of 1889, she did not seek to be an arbitrator or conciliator, helping to bring the strike to an end. She simply launched herself heart and soul into providing the urgent practical help needed to support the strikers and their families in the hardships they faced with no strike pay. Margaret Bondfield, currently leading a campaign for the Women's Co-operative Guild to achieve a minimum wage for women's work, had come to Barton Hill as a Labour trade unionist to support the women's strike. She played a key role in organising it. She was also invited while at Barton Hill to stay at the settlement, which she did. She left without feeling that she had been compromised by this and became a staunch supporter of the settlement, visiting often later to give lectures there.[72] The strike failed but the factory did not

Margaret Bondfield, 1919.

close. It finally closed in the mid–1920s, doomed by competition from factories in Lancashire, Scotland and India.

Meanwhile, the strike had given Cashmore the chance to demonstrate what proved to be one of her greatest personal strengths: an amazing capacity to organise people and resources under the pressure of a crisis. She did this effectively, quickly and on a flexible basis, often with minimum resources, by managing teams of volunteers, playing to their strengths and leaving them with clearly specified tasks to perform, while inspiring their continued support. Soup kitchens and feeding, especially the children, became a priority. Settlement volunteers rallied: Dr Lily Baker, a pioneer qualified doctor who was living in Bristol, offered medical assistance[73] and Miss Walter, a trained nurse and infant welfare worker, provided backup. All settlement workers and extra volunteers worked around the clock visiting homes. In the course of this work, more general issues facing families became clear: the need for support of mothers, antenatal and postpartum; care of infants and sick children, especially those suffering from tuberculosis; support for young people; support for all seeking to gain employment and support of the old. Cashmore was defining the local social needs that the settlement should address, by campaigning for more state assistance and by providing what was possible through voluntary work.

Training social workers and initiating new social services

In this period, local knowledge in the hugely disparate economic regions of Britain could be, potentially, a very effective way of building social policies by adapting the relationship between the local government and voluntary organisations, to ensure that public institutions and voluntary action worked together.[74] Cashmore was ready to give it a try. After the strike, she experimented with the idea of being an 'objective third party' in Bristol, operating between the publicly funded and voluntary relief agencies, helping to keep communication channels open between them and giving a voice for people excluded by any of the bodies. She formed contacts with local government officials at all levels and sat on committees that already had a mix of representatives of local government and voluntary institutions, for example, the Care Committee of the county-based Local Education Authority. Cashmore was able to make the settlement a local centre for the LEA Care Committee. An example of the kind of work that the settlement could undertake here was organising volunteers to visit children suffering from tuberculosis. By helping mothers and families cope with the extra burden of nursing a sick child, the voluntary workers could listen to their worries, establish exactly what kind of help was needed and bring this knowledge back to the settlement, which could then lobby for local government funds and specific voluntary donations.

This was demonstrated by an independent new initiative that Cashmore launched from the settlement, an Open-Air School for sick children, helped by another donation from Mabel Tothill, who provided a local site on which to house the school. With other donors, and volunteers in the neighbourhood with building skills, they created and equipped a large wooden shed with a broad veranda where beds could be put outside. Children were given a good meal every day (malnourishment being a critical problem) and their health was professionally monitored.[75] With its success, the costs were taken over by the local authority, a relief to the financial resources of the settlement. Government support, however, was slower on another initiative towards improving mother and baby care. The settlement set up a School for Mothers in Barton Hill and another at Moorfields. The most competent social service students were sent to offer their services, and supervised health care was given under the watchful eyes of the settlement's volunteer professionals, Dr Lily Baker and Miss Walter. Cashmore then moved to make this initiative citywide and eventually succeeded by playing a leading part in creating a new co-ordinating body: the voluntary Bristol Infant Welfare Association. There was more backing for these developments from the state after the First World War.

From the start, Cashmore was clear about her key ambitions for the settlement. She had three major social policy objectives. First and foremost, she wanted provision of education for men and women excluded by the state system and, especially for women, training for social work of all kinds. Secondly, she wanted to pioneer the development of new initiatives within the fast-evolving state and voluntary welfare systems, often in collaboration with others, to make sure that these projects got off the ground in Bristol and attract whatever funding was available. Finally, at this stage in the development, she was concerned about the physical, mental and emotional well-being of everyone from the staff and students at the settlement to all the citizens of Barton Hill.

In pursuit of her first objective, the settlement had started in a general way to create an educational environment to encourage such

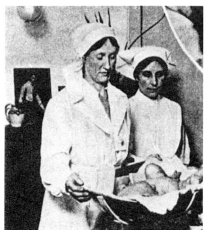

Mothers and babies: "How shall we start making friends with our neighbours?" asked Miss Tothill. [Cashmore's] answer was characteristic. "You and I both love children. We will start with them."

activities. It was given a head start in the provision of adult education, building on the contacts and work of Professor George Hare Leonard, a stalwart supporter of the settlement, who served on its Council. He happened also to be President of the regional branch of the Workers Educational Association, which facilitated organisational meetings, as well as classes, being held at the settlement.[76] The settlement sported a small library in what was called the Toynbee Room, which became the official centre of the East Bristol branch of the WEA. It meant that the settlement became an important hub for the WEA and, as such, Albert Mansbridge, founder of the WEA, a west countryman from Gloucester, was a frequent visitor.[77] Cashmore did not wait for people to come to the settlement; she was prepared to reach out across the city and responded warmly to all invitations to give educational lectures to trade unions (usually restricted in membership to men only) and other groups, mostly on modern economic and social history. Often, she was the first woman to be invited by them to give public lectures. Of course, she also strongly supported the Women's Co-operative Society and encouraged them in their educational work. She developed close links and mutual support between the settlement and the Women's Co-operative Guild on key social issues, such as her campaign to force Bristol local government to take up the issue of providing new social housing.

Cashmore was particularly concerned about the future of younger working women, for whom education after the age of 10 was not an option. Starting with the young women of Barton Hill she resurrected the idea of a girls' club, as the earlier one run by Marian Pease had faded in the 1890s.[78] She was able to interest the girls in coming to the settlement on a regular basis by providing a recreational space for them that they enjoyed, but she could not persuade them to take seriously the idea of further education that might lead to training for new jobs. She tried very hard to overcome this (possibly) culturally determined, but certainly practical, attitude of the young women, given their economic and social circumstances. She offered free refreshments of tea and cakes. She got extra funding from the Local Education Authority, now officially responsible for developing continuing education. She set up an experiment in making her weekly meeting with young women part of the Barton Hill Evening Continuation School. This did produce some results. The classes held at the settlement were initially a great success but eventually interest fell away. All activities at the settlement were self-governing, the essential pre-requisite for social equality, and the Settlement Girls' Club members themselves decided they no longer wanted any education, they just wanted to come to the settlement as they loved the recreational activities.[79]

Cashmore, though, did not give up the idea of getting older women interested in taking this path to new employment. Under the 1918 Education Act, day continuation courses were given a boost. Using her experience from the Women's Day Training College, she took the opportunity of setting up a course through the university, though held at the settlement, to train women to become teachers on these courses, mainly devoted to social work. She was able to secure further funding, given to the settlement independently of the university, for practical training in this. Under her supervision, student teachers were given tuition on "the principles and practice of social work from an educational point of view".[80]

However, the major emphasis on education and training as one of the primary functions of the settlement gradually took shape around training mainly women for new prospects in social work of all kinds. This is what Cashmore and Pease had wanted for their students at the university and for women interested in this kind of work across the city. The major task of the first two years of the settlement was setting up appropriate courses, some general, some theoretical but also a range of options that gave students the chance to gain the practical experience that could lead to paid work. The result of these efforts was the putting together of a number of courses which could collectively earn the certificate validated by the university, the Social Study Testamur.[81] University validation gave the Testamur the status of a professional qualification. Cashmore's training for her social studies students offered a mix of practical and theoretical elements as a grounding to whatever specialism they wanted to follow afterwards.

The key characteristic of the Bristol Social Study Testamur rested on Cashmore's belief that training for social work should have a large practical content, hands-on experience, up-to-date practical knowledge that could give a clear understanding of what could be achieved and how to achieve it. There were seven training objectives, with practical work having the edge over academic study, though that was not neglected. Students were expected to undertake: visits to institutions in the city, factories as well as local government departments concerned with social issues; practical techniques of research, organising and keeping records; experience of educational and recreational work; voluntary work with civic agencies; Mothers' School and Infant Welfare work; Industrial Welfare Work and work with the Play Centre Organisation under the Board of Education. This kind of training provided women students who might in the past had attended the Higher-Grade School Board Schools some kind of secondary education which could open up opportunities for professional careers, most of which had been male preserves up to this time.

There was a graded range of opportunities based on educational backgrounds, which included official inspectors of many kinds such as those for factories and public health. With more medical training, there were strong possibilities for becoming professional state-authorised midwives or undertaking neighbourhood work for infant-life protection, with qualifications based on courses at the settlement, or inspecting the care of boarded-out children. Other possibilities included some poor law work or educational work—the list was being continuously extended. Much was possible for women with some secondary education but for women without that, settlement courses could open up possibilities, especially if students had shown a willingness to try day continuation schools and relevant evening classes. More jobs were becoming available with both government agencies and commercial firms, especially departmental stores and

SOCIAL STUDY TESTAMUR.

The Warden of the Settlement is responsible for the organisation of the work of the University students in the practice of social work. The syllabus for which the Settlement makes itself responsible includes the following :—

1. **Visits to Institutions.** Some fifteen of these visits take place, and include visits to such Institutions as
    Employment Bureaux.
    Poor Law Institutions.
    Police Courts.
    Factories and Workshops.
    Educational Institutions.
    Hospitals and Dispensaries, both General and Special.
    Public Health Works.

2. **Office Work and Relief Work.**
    Business methods in social work.
    Correspondence and Indexing.
    The keeping of simple accounts.
    The use of case papers.
    How to use existing agencies.
    Principles of decision.

3. **Educational and Recreational Work.** This includes work for two terms in some class or club, and the necessary reading and organisation in connection with it.

4. **Voluntary work in connection with Civic Agencies.** Visiting in connection with the Juvenile Advisory Committees, visiting for the Voluntary Committee, for the Care Committee of the Education Committee.

5. **Mothers' School and Infant Welfare Work.**

6. **Industrial Welfare Work.**

7. **Play Centre Organisation under the Board of Education.**

Students work under a Tutor, and much opportunity is given for discussion of the principles underlying the various experiments which are studied.

Eleven students undertook the work. Six presented themselves for examination for the First Examination, and we congratulate the following on their success in satisfying the examiners :—

Miss BUDDEN   Miss PORTEOUS   Miss ORPEN
Miss CARTER   Miss WARREN

Training of Infant Welfare Workers. In these two years the Settlement Association has further developed a scheme for training Infant Welfare Workers. Our special aim was to secure, that while the students have careful training in the preventive and educational Health work of the schools, they should also have some real insight into the conditions of life under which our people are compelled to live, and some study of the principles of Constructive Social Reform. For this reason we have insisted on residence at the Settlement for at least a year. The course has been approved by the London Sanitary Institute, which body has recognised the Settlement as a centre for the training of Health Visitors. The course has received the full approval of the Medical Officer of Health, and the social principles for which the Settlement has stood are winning ground in the wider fields of training. The students working at the Settlement spend one year of their course at the British Hospital for mothers and babies, Woolwich, where they are prepared for the examination of the Central Midwives' Board, and by special arrangement are carefully instructed in the problems of ante-natal work and post-natal work, and of infant feeding, up to school age. This connection of the Settlement School for Mothers with one of the best Training Schools for midwives in the country, has done an incalculable amount towards the establishment and maintenance of the high standard of our schools.

We congratulate the following residents on their success :—

Miss LEILA STOCK, San. Inst. Final S. for M. Exam.
Miss MARGARET SMITH, Health Visitor's Certificate.
Miss ROSSITER   ,,   ,,   ,,
Miss BRAITHWAITE, Sen. Inst. Final S. for M. Exam.
Miss WHITE   ,,   ,,   ,,
Miss SHEWELL   ,,   ,,   ,,
Miss ROBERT, Health Visitor's Certificate.

We offer special congratulations to Miss Shewell, who, in the three years she was with us as Nursing Superintendent of the Barton Hill Mothers' School, took her Health Visitor's Certificate and her Heads for Schools for Mothers' Certificate. She has now resigned her appointment here, to the great regret of the school, to take up a larger sphere of work in Birmingham.

Social Study Testamur.

local offices, starting to recruit more women. Cashmore concentrated on initiatives that could lead into professional careers at varied levels. Through her sister Maud, she had already set up a partnership between the settlement and the British Hospital for Mothers and Babies in Woolwich, to give students on the Testamur course in Bristol practical nursing experience.[82] The students who took this course could apply for jobs as health visitors, heads of schools for mothers, or undertake further training to become midwives.

Recognition of these developments came from national and local bodies: for example, the London Sanitary Institute approved the settlement course for the training of health visitors, and Bristol's Medical Officer of Health gave his approval for those based in Bristol. As the government-prescribed framework of social services evolved, Cashmore's hope was that the influence of the settlement's reputation for social work training would attract students from wider afield. She did indeed attract students from elsewhere in the UK, with the reputation for excellence of the Testamur qualification, ratified by the university, being widely recognised, with some of its alumni going on to achieve careers on the national stage. Two outstanding examples of her success in this were Dorothy Johnson and Grace Drysdale. Dorothy Johnson, a student resident at the settlement during the war, actually took the course that Cashmore prepared for training welfare workers in industry. From there she went to the local Robinson's factory as welfare officer and then got the nationally based job of HM Deputy Chief Inspector of Factories. Grace Drysdale, who had met Cashmore in London in the early 1920s and came to Bristol for her training, wrote in the Memorial volume: "it was quite obvious to me that Hilda Cashmore was the leader of the settlement movement in Britain and when I decided to train for my Diploma in Social Studies, I asked to be sent to Bristol for my practical training".[83] In 1944 Drysdale became the Deputy Secretary of the Scottish Council of Social Service, and a key figure in the future development of that organisation.[84]

A flourishing settlement and the challenges of the First World War

Hilda Cashmore was the driving force behind the achievements mentioned in the previous section. However, the one thing that is very difficult to discover is what she was like and how people responded to her. She, like many Quakers, had an abhorrence of self-aggrandisement of any kind and never claimed responsibility for her successes, always keen to pay tribute to the importance of the contributions of others. Her friends were ready to claim, though, that her extreme personal reticence, even shyness, had been evident since childhood and that this shyness did not hold her back from vigorously tackling all the challenges she faced. Jessie Noakes, an undergraduate with her at Somerville, Oxford, who knew her all her adult life, commented on what she found most impressive about her:

> her unbounded energy, fiery life—she always seemed ready and able to do a little more than anyone else... Coupled with this was an overflowing sympathy and consideration for others... (she) always knew how best to offer help, and mercifully with it all was a delightful sense of humour.[85]

In the absence of her letters-though she was an inveterate letter writer and kept in touch with many friends—this section will try to offer insights into her character and personality by looking at her own words, her actions and finally, a personal perspective. These sources comprise the text of a surviving published lecture, her minutes of the special meeting of the University Settlement Association in 1919 and some perceptive comments on her way of working from Winifred Gill who worked with her in Bristol and Manchester. Her own special contributions to the war effort will be covered, too, giving another viewpoint of her achievements. The First World War was to mark a critical period for the settlement and even more so for Hilda Cashmore personally. She was to apply for two periods of leave at the beginning and end of the war so that she could contribute personally to the Friends' War Victims Relief Committee, at the start in France, at the end in Poland. At the outbreak of war in 1914, she had just completed five years of continuous work at the settlement without a break.

She was aware that the role of the settlement would become dramatically changed in wartime, but she also felt a huge personal desire to help those civilian victims whose lives had got caught up as war swept through their homes and communities. As soon as war was declared, she applied for six months leave which she was given by the university and the settlement committee, who thought she needed a break to get ready for what was to come. She, meanwhile, had quietly conceived a personal plan. She promptly left for London, to enrol on the very first mission to France of the pioneering Friends' War Victims Relief Committee, demonstrating her Quaker belief in the futility of war and the need to help all those non-combatants whose lives had been affected.[86] She was not able to support the peace movement openly as a warden but that only made Cashmore all the more determined to show that she cared about the effects of war, by doing what she could to help victims. The Friends' War Victims Relief Committee was set up in 1914 in London at the instigation of Dr Hilda Clark, a member of the Quaker shoe manufacturing dynasty in Chard, Somerset, and was led by T Edmund Harvey, recently retired from the position of warden of Toynbee Hall and currently a Liberal MP in London.

Clark had trained as a doctor and like Cashmore had been especially influenced by the leadership of JW Rowntree, attending his special summer schools. It is highly likely that they were friends, though there is no extant evidence of this. By going to France with the Quaker Relief Group in November 1914, Cashmore was to be in at the very beginning of an extraordinary organisation that was to expand enormously over the next four years to reach millions of civilians caught up in the war, to an extent undreamed of in the early days. She also took with her her young colleague, Lettice Jowitt, the third resident of Bristol University Settlement and lecturer in Social Studies at the university, who wanted to be involved.[87] Cashmore was to leave for France on the 6th November and returned in May 1915. She found it a hugely moving experience. This pioneer Quaker group was well set up to deal with whatever they found. It contained people with different skills including "three doctors, ten nurses, ambulance men and drivers with cars, an architect, two chemists and a sanitary inspector".[88] It needed to, as these were the winter months and many of the refugees had inappropriate clothing, little shelter and needed food supplies.

Hilda was given the crucial primary task of interfacing with the people they wished to help, the refugees and civilians themselves, and directing the appropriate help to them.[89] This was no easy task, as numbers changed all the time, and it was not easy to prioritise the most urgent things and to work alongside the people themselves to do this. In this task, she was at the nub of the whole enterprise since connecting with the people was the primary objective. Cashmore had been chosen for this role because of her huge talent in engaging with war victims, communicating with them sympathetically and gaining their confidence.[90] She spoke French fluently. When Cashmore returned to England her role was to be taken over between 1915–17 by Margery Fry and her sister Ruth. Margery became famous for her work, as the scale of the Quaker relief mission grew to major proportions. Her sister Ruth was to be the historian of the Quaker relief movement, collecting the statistics and providing an account of what took place in her volume, *A Quaker Adventure*, published later in 1926.[91]

Cashmore, during her stay, helped to deal with the flood of refugee civilians in the north of France who had virtually nothing as they had had to flee suddenly because of the fighting. Food, shelter and warmth were essential in the cold temperatures. There were old people, young families and pregnant mothers, many sick men and women, all very vulnerable as the winter set in. She witnessed at first-hand how a small group of dedicated people could be undaunted by the size of the challenge of helping significant numbers of traumatised and destitute individuals and communities, and could succeed, often beyond expectation. Obviously, this was during a war, but she saw it as an example of how the intensity of the desire to help, to be found amongst the Quaker Committee, was like a "red hot" force for good. She was to use this phrase herself when, over a decade later, she was campaigning to make the settlement movement a way of facilitating social transformation in a Britain of divided politics and a hugely unequal society.

She came back to Britain in May 1915, as trench warfare had set in in northern France, aware of the disparity between the British and Germans in the effectiveness of their weapons. The Germans had better guns. By 1916 there was a change of Prime Minister to Lloyd George, and under his initiative, the Whitehall bureaucracy was expanded to include a new *ad hoc* Ministry of Munitions. This extraordinary Ministry was tasked with redesigning and improving Britain's munitions and it had a different structure from the normal ministries then in place. It could break rules because of the urgent need to respond to getting troops on the front supplied with weaponry that could equal that of the enemy. Businessmen were recruited to serve because of their knowledge of where to find resources and how to organise production; press barons were asked to communicate what was happening in their newspapers so as to drum up support in the country; new factories were built at breakneck speed and, alongside them, new housing for the munition workers. It was fast and it was mainly successful in terms of output, but the price of speed and lack of management experience was paid for by the many social problems affecting the workers, especially the heavily recruited women workers.

Cashmore had come back to the large workload of her duties at the settlement, but she was also keenly aware of the problems of women in war work since some of this was taking place in front of her in Bristol. Her first priority was the Barton Hill neighbourhood, but she did not lose sight of the new development of the munition factories. At the settlement she found challenging circumstances that magnified as the war progressed. Many families and individuals were suffering severe social problems with widespread unemployment and sickness and also large-scale local emergencies. In the latter category were two major epidemics: of measles in 1918 and the pandemic of influenza, 1918–19. Extra support drummed up included the settlement doctor, Dr Lily Baker, and the services of Miss Walter initially, though towards the end of the war Dr Baker offered her services to the military and poor Miss Walter succumbed fatally to influenza.[92] Hilda managed to find two volunteer doctors willing to take their place. There was also a need to raise money for food for the families affected. This was no mean feat as the numbers involved were considerable: in one month alone, for example, special help was given to 60 families and the same was needed for different families in subsequent periods. She was touched and delighted that the people being helped also wanted to give whatever they could to the settlement to help others. It was a true indication of community spirit from the people.

Key concerns were first of all the children. The war had brought much more financial support with government grants for settlement activities in respect of children and she swung into action to apply for them. Funds were available to deal with a number of key health issues, the health of mothers as well as their babies and young children and especially the feeding of school children. George Newman, Chief Medical Officer of Health and architect of these national policies wrote: "The School Medical Service has emerged from the War... As a result of the War there has arisen a new conception of the value of the child to the nation".[93] The Bristol Settlement had been working towards this since its inception. But Cashmore had not forgotten the women war workers, now another challenge in Bristol since munition factories were being built there. What protection did they have in their working conditions? There were new estates being built to house the workers but little effort to provide social services for the ordinary business of living. Cashmore could see that the welfare of the munition workers could become a settlement activity through developing training schemes to send qualified people to offer substantial support.

The need for this had been recognised on a national scale, wherever new factories were being established. The lack of concern over the welfare of the workers had been made clear to the government as a national scandal had erupted over the treatment of women undertaking war work in munition factories. In response to this, a Health and Welfare of Munition Workers Committee was created in the Ministry of Munitions and eventually Lloyd George persuaded BS Rowntree to chair it. Rowntree found it an uphill struggle to implement change since, as Gail Braybon has written: "the government was not prepared to step in to protect women working with TNT or aircraft dope, or make sure they received financial reward for the risks they ran".[94] But one recommendation was quickly taken up. Firms were required by law to appoint welfare supervisors to oversee matters to do with the health and welfare of the workforce. Here was Cashmore's chance and she responded to it quickly. This law could be a recipe for disaster if there was no accepted training for such posts or even clear expectations of what they should do. Such welfare supervisors needed training and she could provide courses at the settlement.

To launch her project, she wrote a paper, *The Possibilities of Industrial Welfare Work as a New Profession for Women*.[95] This was published as a pamphlet and is the first of her published documents to have survived, providing a rare glimpse of Cashmore's own voice. It is worth looking at this paper in depth, as it gives an authentic insight into her personal views. She writes not only about industrial welfare work for women but also about the role of welfare work generally, and specifically on what experiences are needed for creating new industrial welfare policies that could be successful. She points out, using deliberately incongruous details, how an imposition, such as this *dictat* by the Ministry of Munitions, constructing a new law without thinking it through, simply demonstrates how out of touch government could be with both management and workers. She quotes from a survey 'an amusing list' of people who had been appointed as welfare workers under this legislation, made by a Miss Pond. They included: "clergymen, teachers, organists, doctors, gymnasts, overlookers, cooks, ex-constables and some workers from the shopfloor".[96]

In her paper Cashmore wanted to hammer home the following points: that trained women welfare workers are an immediate answer; that welfare workers are used extensively in the most modern factories in the USA, adopting the new 'scientific management' now followed by progressive employers in the UK, obviously including the Cadburys and Rowntrees, albeit rather slowly—the first two conferences on industrial welfare work in England were in 1909 and 1913 in Birmingham and York;[97] and finally that the welfare worker, while not having any role in industrial disputes, could have a role in helping workers and capitalists to recognise a need to work "with greater unity of aim in the direction and development of their industry as a whole". She is entirely practical and writes in a vigorous and forceful style, ready to take on possible objections to her proposals. She sees major obstacles as "all the prejudices of factory life", especially those towards women, even from male trade unionists, and that this could feed into hostility to the idea of women welfare officers. It is a hostility aroused also by the fact that the role hinted at 'do-goodery' and there was a "deep suspicion of philanthropy which is inherent in the modern view of life."

She states firmly that: "the age for this beneficence of charity extended from one class to another beneath it has gone, there is a cry for justice and not charity now" and that the work of the welfare officer is just a step towards this. The task of negotiating pay is a union matter. The task of the welfare worker is to address the effects of new methods of production on the health and well-being of the worker:

> When implemented this might give a chance, at least sometimes, of Management and the Workpeople working together with greater unity of aim in the direction and development of their industry as a whole.

Always seeking new job opportunities for her students, Cashmore wants to promote the idea of this work for university women—the only women at this time likely to have had secondary education. She suggests:

> A young woman, with the heart of a philanthropist and the head of a student, would find it an admirable exercise, for a year or so after her year of theoretical social study, and as a preliminary to work as a Factory Inspector, or a Board of Trade Official. Again, it might be an invaluable business training.

She is not afraid to say that it might encourage at least some university women, "to become employers of labour—instead of staying at home and leaving all that kind of thing to their brothers", suggesting that French women are not held back by prejudices of class and status.

But beyond mapping future possibilities for her students, she reveals in this paper a longer-term perspective on future changes, new ways that might be better for workers and capitalists and government. She is even prepared to say that perhaps 'welfare officers' are not the way forward. She has sympathy with the labour suspicion that the welfare officer may appear to act as the "paid spy of the management".[98] She saw that making it a legal requirement to appoint welfare officers in factories during the war was possibly clutching at straws in a moment of crisis and that, in the longer term, it was probably ill-advised. A good alternative approach, she believes, if properly set up, may work for labour and management: get rid of the idea of a welfare officer altogether, "it is an experiment warranted by the exigencies of a time of crisis." Work out which government department should be responsible for particular needs: the sick require the "functions of a trained nurse ... a caterer and general supervisor of dining and rest arrangements, might be grafted onto the requirements of the Factory Department, and cause no more dispute than in the past".

Her proposal was that there should be a proper 'welfare' department composed of representatives of employers, trade union officials and educationalists under the direction of the Board of Education. She envisages that such a department in each factory would concentrate on working conditions and the aspirations of the workers. Her vision of a welfare department is one devoted to the present and future interests of the workers, not one acting as a tool of management. She suggested the Board of Education should be made responsible for this work, as a suitably disinterested body, uninvolved in direct conflicts of interest between management and workers, yet still a government department that could oversee and regulate good practice and provide resources. This would give factory welfare departments a chance to keep the interests of the workers at its heart. She was well informed about the growth of the labour movement and the struggle between labour and capital. She also saw that: "the divergence between the interests of Labour and Capital, the slow organisation of two hostile forces would reappear with a vengeance after the war". But she hangs on to the hope that:

the awful results of war have burnt themselves into this generation, and the idealism of the best leaders on either side points to a searching after the consciousness of an eventual community of interest between masters and men, with a wise Government as arbitrator.[99]

She was writing before the Russian Revolution and the aftermath of war in Europe marked by revolutionary activities in many European cities and, across Europe, the complete dislocation of industry, trade and finance. This was to be coupled in Britain with the progressive decline of those basic staple industries that had sustained the country: coal mining, iron and steel, textiles and heavy engineering, which would bring the scourge of the future: unemployment. But she was not being totally idealistic. Ever practical, her improvised, pioneering, shortened social studies course for welfare workers in factories was successful and gained national recognition. Cashmore was to take every opportunity produced by the war to extend her voluntary activities in wider areas for the social benefit of all.

Building on the experiences of her war work in France as well as at Barton Hill, she set up another new course of basic social work training for local officials and social workers on how to deal with families and neighbourhoods in times of a crisis or in an emergency. This was designed to work beyond the normal emergency services of fire, police and ambulance. Her target was to deal with the dislocation brought to the surrounding area and local people in some unexpected catastrophe. She was thinking of war, pandemics, starvation or accidental civic disasters. This activity brought her into contact with city councillors, Labour Exchange officials, large employers and voluntary social agencies who began to be willing to work with the settlement. She immediately sent students to these institutions and industries to gain new experiences.

What she brought to these initiatives was the confidence that she had set up a unique and strong institutional structure at the settlement and there were bodies of committed people who supported her. It is worth exploring this support in more detail as it was the essence of her belief in the importance of voluntary work for the present and future and how voluntary settlements mattered because they could create services for people either beyond or more quickly than the state. It is also an indication of her personal actions, reflecting her character and personality. The organisation of the settlement was based on three overlapping but still distinct groups that brought great flexibility (and minimal bureaucracy), enabling her to pursue her objectives and respond quickly when chances for future activities presented themselves. There was the small Settlement Executive Committee which could act quickly; the Settlement Residents' Association which was in touch with the different branches of activity within the settlement; and the Association of Settlement Members who could respond immediately with practical support and labour to get things done.

This latter group included everyone from volunteer students, members of groups involved in settlement activities (particularly the WEA), donors and basically anyone who wanted to get involved further in settlement matters. Alderman Cunningham told the last warden of the settlement, Hilda Jennings, many years later in 1937 when she took office: "remember, it is not the Warden or the Residents who make the Settlement, but the members".[100] It was a tribute to the strength of the institutional structure that Cashmore had created and the long-lasting loyalties that this had engendered. These Settlement bodies came together usually on an annual basis but during the war, two years had to be elided into one meeting: a Special Settlement Council Meeting covering two years, 1917–1919. The normal annual meeting had a regular format when the financial accounts were presented and the activities over the year in question reported on. In this meeting, the discussion was wider, taking in the effects of the war and the challenges of the future.

The minutes of this meeting have happened to survive, and their idiosyncratic presentation demonstrates a dynamic rarely found in records of such proceedings. It is clear that Cashmore, as the Hon. Secretary of the Association, wrote them, and she was able to present her account of how she saw the settlement functioning in the present and the preparation for future challenges. The Council met on 19th September 1919 under the chairmanship of the President of both the Settlement Council and the Settlement Executive Committee, Professor Lloyd Morgan, the last president of University College Bristol. He had retired when Bristol had got its charter in 1909 to make way for the first new vice-chancellor, but he had continued ever since faithfully to support the settlement. The meeting began on a sad note, to record the deaths of Professor Arthur Skemp, who had run the boys' club, a strong supporter of the settlement, and organiser of many amateur theatrical entertainments, who had given much time to the settlement, killed in France in November 1918, and also that of Miss Evelyn Walter, the senior nurse who had been made Hon. Superintendent of the Schools for Mothers and who had given huge personal service to the settlement in times of crisis. She died in November 1918, having been very active in nursing the sick in the measles and influenza outbreaks at Barton Hill when she caught pneumonia followed by influenza, during the great influenza pandemic.

The next agenda item also made dismal reading: the Treasurer's Report. The settlement had suffered a regular annual deficit of £200 over several years that had accumulated. Educational activities, clubs and societies, some partly supported by grants from the state, only survived because residents and friends had given an extra £315 that was not charged to the general subscription list. The war had produced more official grants, especially for the mothers' schools and the Open-Air School, but the settlement finances were tight. This deficit had been a perennial problem, but the loyalty of subscribers somehow kept the settlement able to function.

The minutes continue on a much more upbeat note, the main heading concerning the settlement's activities with the title: 'Study of Social and Educational Work and Experience'. This all-embracing section has three sub-sections: industrial conditions in a period of transition from war to peace; the problems raised by the 1918 Education Act, especially problems of recreation and continued education; and problems of housing and town planning. These were all issues that were city-wide, and the ensuing text strongly reflects this, even in its 'official' form, demonstrating the optimism under duress of the minute-taker. Under 'Industrial Conditions' there is a report of first-hand studies of problems. The first is the state of the city's economy and the question of employment conditions when in work, and of course the prospect of unemployment in post-war conditions. Mention is made of the training of industrial welfare workers and it says that settlement residents and students had been working in factories "in London, Bristol, Melksham, Cardiff, Wellington, Coventry, Hereford and Sheffield".

In 1918 the Executive of the Central Association of Industrial Welfare Workers (presumably government backed) held their weekend meeting at the Bristol Settlement. Leading factories and workshops in Bristol had opened their doors to settlement students and so had Bristol Labour Exchange. Members of the Bristol Reconstruction Committee and Organisers of Women's Labour had given opportunities for the study of women's industrial problems. Hilda records that a member of the settlement (in fact herself) had been appointed to the new Trades Boards for tobacco, corsets and paper bags; and the sub-warden had been appointed to the Munitions Tribunals for Bristol and the Western Counties. Her concern for the future employment possibilities for women is evident.

Her next sub-section on educational work continued in the same positive vein, mention being made of continuing education and the difference the 1918 Act will make to this, which will especially benefit women. The settlement had already had three resident students who had undertaken a special course of study in training, now funded by government. It was based round her own work on the study of the principles and practice of social work from an educational point of view. The pride of place in the minutes on education at the settlement is naturally given to the Social Study Testamur. This appears to be flourishing and these minutes give some insight into how some of the activities were functioning. No exact numbers are given of the students but eleven take one course and seven, all named, have been successful over all the courses and been awarded the Testamur. The 'jewel in the crown' of the settlement's work was in good heart even during wartime. Other educational work was also flourishing and wide ranging, such as the Working Girls Winter School at Penscot. Cashmore had taught regularly on this throughout that winter, taking with her four working girls from Barton Hill: one a worker from a corset factory, one from a tobacco factory and two young female trade union organisers. There was also a student from an aeroplane factory in Birmingham who then became a resident at the settlement. Lectures were given to a wide range of audiences, across Bristol and the West Country, touching the Midlands, and of course, in London (many by Cashmore herself) and a list gives some indication of this work.[101]

There was also another agenda slot for 'Educational and Social Work in the Immediate Neighbourhood of the Settlement Houses and in Surrounding Districts'. Much of this is concerned with preventive and educational health work in infant clinics, the municipal ante-natal clinic and the social and club life of young mothers, which includes domestic science classes, lectures, clothing club and other activities. Usually, much of the work improving the health of mothers had been undertaken by Dr Lily Baker but she had left Bristol to take up military work. Two replacement doctors, Dr Falconar and Dr Winifred Austin, had taken over. The next big topic was the work among the children. Top of the list here is the Open-Air School. Another new development highlighted was after care visiting of all juveniles in the local area, from when they left school until they reach 16 years old. This is mostly to support them in getting employment by just keeping in touch, as well as providing encouragement and advice. Lists go on in a mind-blowing quantity: school visitors work and training (including becoming school managers); care committee in respect of medical inspection of school children; play-centres at Barton Hill and Moorfields (in the summer); children's library; summer camp—sixth form of Sidcot School usually invited ten children to stay at school camp, but in 1918 this was not possible, so the Sidcot girls came to the settlement for a week to look after the children on holiday from school.

There is an important and upbeat section devoted to the recreational work undertaken by the settlement: lots of social clubs for many different groups, summer camps for boys, the settlement hut at Cleeve for families. There was not as much as usual because of the war but Cashmore believed strongly that recreation was essential not just for fun but for mental health and wellbeing, and if possible should be connected to nature, not just for health and happiness of settlement workers but for everyone else as well. She regularly took groups of earnest young teachers or settlement volunteers on reading parties and country walking to nearby places in the Quantocks or further away in Devon, many times with small parties, using Marian Pease's country cottage for overnight stays, sometimes extending to study weeks. She forged friendships and connections that lasted a lifetime—as evident in the Memorial volume.[102] The Settlement Association minutes describe one of her favourite events, the May Festival which took place for the whole community in Barton Hill in 1919, and Cashmore reports that the May Day procession was longer than ever. It was the closest way Cashmore could connect her inner city to nature. Winifred Gill's account of it shows Hilda's delight in this and how much she cared:

The May Festival… was the children's day and they went nearly wild with excitement as one familiar step followed another in a crescendo of enchantment, leading up to the great day itself, a Saturday in May. The full glory of the festival began on the Friday with the arrival all day long of boxes, hampers and trunks of cowslips, bluebells, orchids, campion, branches of blossom, and

Barton Hill Whitsun Festival 1930s.

boughs of young beech. Bands of important children went the rounds of the streets borrowing galvanised baths from willing neighbours—twenty, thirty, forty, sometimes fifty were needed to hold the numbers of little bunches of flowers till the floor of the big hall [at the Settlement] would be covered. Hilda always looked in for a few minutes before the hall was locked up for the night, to enjoy the beauty of it. Saturday morning passed in breathless activity … At last all was ready: the band to head the procession, the Girl Guides to set the pace slow enough for the little ones, the small May Queen with her trainbearers and attendants followed by the whole Play Centre dressed in bright tabards and carrying banners and flowered wands … There was one supreme moment when the police held up the traffic on the high road, even the trams, to let the procession pass. There was no one happier than Hilda herself, as she moved up and down the little procession humming a little tune.[103]

The 1919 minutes flagged up a growing concern that was to involve Cashmore more and more: the question of housing and its condition in the inner city and also the building of estates at the city's periphery. Her thoughts on this were evolving and will be explored in the next section. Winifred Gill, however, made a pertinent comment about Hilda that pinpoints her role in all the activities at the settlement and her personal vision. She wrote: "Hilda was a superb organiser, and in looking to the future, she laid her plans on a broad scale. She made use of existing organisations and linked her work with that of municipal and national bodies, thus guarding the Settlement from being parochial".[104] The 1919 Minutes gives ample evidence of this.

After the war, there was another important interlude in her life. She applied for some leave in 1920 after another five years without a break and was to go again to Europe with the Quakers, this time to Poland for three months. She had become deeply concerned about the conditions of civilians in the continuing war between Russia and Poland, especially the peasants who were fleeing and were without any support. Outbreaks of typhus were widespread, and she volunteered to nurse the suffering. The situation she was to find herself in was a far cry from even the desperate conditions she had experienced in France in the winter of 1914–15. There was chaos in every respect as war and civil war raged still unresolved. The trains they had to travel by, since there was no motor traffic and few roads in the countryside could take them anyway, were full of Polish soldiers going to the front and many were refugees, old Russians trying to leave now that their land, after some decades, was no longer in Poland. She describes "stations full of soldiers and Polish peasants in costume and ancient Russian men in canvas shoes and a kind of red carpet coat, carrying enormous burdens on their backs, primitive beyond anything one had believed and *so* dirty".

Writing to Marian Pease, she tries to give an insight of what all the peasants were facing with the history of a single Polish family in detail:

they had fled for hundreds of miles, they lost two or three of their family on the way; then they lived for years amongst strangers, then they trekked back to find not one stone on another and their holding unrecognisable in the general waste except to their own eyes. Then the typhus came and the whole village had it, penned in the bitter cold in these awful little dens, then they had to face the spring with no possibility of working their land, no horses, no seed, no tools, no hope of buying food or clothes, no school for the children to go to.[105]

She found herself working alongside the American and the Polish Red Cross but helping to organise food rather than nursing the typhus victims that she had come to do, until at last, in her last month, June 1920, she was called on for some nursing. The situation by then was very bad, the Russians were beating the Polish soldiers back, and the anti-typhus work was horrible; the heat was intense, and it was not possible to communicate with the suffering because of language barriers. She had met a fellow worker from Bristol, the young Alizon Fox of the Frenchay Quakers, who was in her group. Alizon described in her letters home the extreme difficulties of their tasks but also the daily physical hardships they themselves endured. As a young woman, Alizon was also initially somewhat wary of this warden figure, in her mid-forties, who wore astonishing hats. But Cashmore, as was her wont, downplayed physical hardships and was cheerful whatever the latest difficulties, proving herself immensely capable at her work. They became good friends, dealing with the great difficulties that beset them.[106] It was an astonishing episode in her life and possibly prepared her a little in terms of hardship with what she was later to find in India in the 1930s. However, when she came back to Bristol, she was to continue the work she had outlined in the 1919 minutes.

3. Cashmore's leadership of the settlement movement

Post-war reconstruction and community building
on Bristol's new estates

Bristol had not had much public housing before the war, unlike many other cities that had taken advantage of the 1890 Housing Act permitting, but not mandating, the use of public funds for this. The 1909 Housing and Town Planning Act of the Liberal Government had edged a little closer to compulsion by insisting on the need for plans for the estates that were springing up around cities to serve new industries and population growth.[107] During the war, Bristol experienced some compulsion from the Ministry of Munitions, which had set up new munition industries on the outskirts of the city and needed housing for the workers. The Ministry built an estate at Kings Weston, to house workers for a new munitions factory. The houses were built under the planning regulations being drawn up by the government, which were strongly influenced by the Garden City architect, Raymond Unwin, now the town planning advisor on the Local Government Board.[108] Kings Weston was therefore designed like a mini Bournville, or like New Earswick, for that matter, designed for the Rowntrees by Unwin and his partner, Barry Parker. This was Cashmore's chance to extend the settlement's social remit from the inner to the outer city and into a new environment.

By 1918, the Ministry of Munitions had completed another 150 houses for munition workers at Penpole, Shirehampton. These were later to be assigned to workers for a new factory, the National Spelter Works, and more industrial development was planned after the war and more housing needed for the dockers. The dockers' union had proposed that a public utility company should be formed to deal with the provision of social services there, since neither the ministry nor local government had taken any responsibility for these. The National Spelter Works took the initiative in forming such a company at Kings Weston. The Lord Mayor of Bristol, Alderman Sheppard, a former representative of the Boot and Shoe Operatives Union and long-term member of the university settlement, was made chairman of this new public company.[109] Hilda Cashmore became a member alongside Ernest Bevin, then organiser of the Bristol dockers union, and there was a representative of the National Spelter Works. The Spelter Works was persuaded by Cashmore to let one

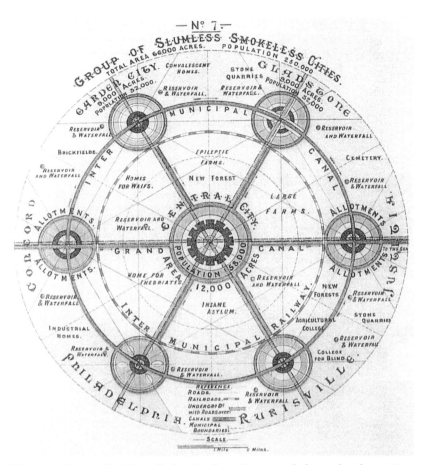

Ebenezer Howard's idea of the Garden City—smokeless, slumless cities made the dream seem realizable.

of the workers' cottages to the university settlement and Miss Ethelwyn Austin, sub-warden and tutor at Barton Hill, went to live there and help to identify demands for appropriate services, in consultation with residents.

In fact, she did not stay long, but her successor, Miss Rotha Clay, remained for the next 23 years, making a huge success of the project. Rotha Clay gave Cashmore practical feedback on what was actually needed in a new neighbourhood and how to deliver it. It was just what Cashmore wanted. She learnt that a trained resident in this situation was able to operate in a democratic way. She could encourage social activities and a demand for services by leaving it to the tenants rather than always initiating or organising them herself. But by being there, and in contact with the university settlement and the local council, she could summon support and extra funding. This was a flexible, appropriate and unpatronizing way forward. However, the next project, also in Shirehampton and Sea Mills, where a further 800 houses were added over the course of the next few years, was not such a total success. Cashmore applied to the Carnegie Trust for funds to employ community workers. She was able to appoint Mr WG Abbott as organising secretary of Shirehampton, Avonmouth and the Sea Mills Community Association. Unfortunately, this was too large an area to weld into a cohesive neighbourhood, or to "foster community activities and promote adult education", which was Mr Abbott's remit.[110] He failed in this larger ambition but settled on developing clubs and societies in the new part of Shirehampton, with the help of two other volunteers. This was a success, and this outpost of the settlement was made an associate committee of the Barton Hill Settlement.

It was the beginning of a system of affiliating new areas to Barton Hill that was to result in three extensions of settlement work in outlying areas.[111] As these ideas crystallised at the end of the war, Cashmore had taken up the cause of making this kind of support with small community centres happen, not only in Bristol, but across the country. It was to be a long haul. First, she was the driving force behind the setting up of a national federation of residential settlements so that they would be given a future voice in the post-war deliberations on voluntary social work in their local areas. What she wanted was community centres in all new development areas. She saw this as best achieved by settlement-supported community centres in rapidly expanding public housing suburbs where there were people who had expertise in facilitating such ventures. Indeed, she thought of it as an important new duty of inner-city residential settlements to support this work.

She had witnessed the growth of Quaker educational settlements, some residential, some not, but all contributing to a powerful boost for the adult education movement and important in building contacts between people. This was what was really needed in new suburbs. Many people, though mostly men at this time, had found adult education not only a hugely rewarding personal experience but also an important stepping-stone towards taking part in public life, in politics, trade unionism and social endeavours.

Cashmore was to argue the importance of meeting this new challenge for settlement work as housing estates mushroomed on the periphery of many cities, large and small. She recognised that the life chances of inhabitants would be dependent on connections at every level because they were cut off from established facilities, from information about available jobs to the city's dance halls where they might meet a partner. The possibilities of personally taking part in any kind of public life in the city, key to getting their voices heard, would be much more difficult. Even basic information was hard to come by, from learning about new kinds of work opportunities, to the provision of essential services in education and medical care for families, and especially facilities for recreation and leisure for boys and girls. Above all, women, single and married, needed up-to-date knowledge and contacts to help them make the best of living in such a different environment. Cashmore continued to work tirelessly for the establishment of community associations that were properly funded and connected to other organisations in the city.

She believed this really was the future that had already been predicted by the American Quaker, Mary Parker Follett, whose work she had come across in Chicago on her research trip in 1911 and whose fame in the US had continued to grow rapidly.[112] In Britain, Cashmore could be seen as a pioneer. In Leicestershire, the claim is made that the pioneer of community centres was Charles Booth who, with his wife, established a rural community centre in his home village of Thringstone in 1903, for use by all villages in the surrounding areas. But that was really an update of parish activities in the village hall, a venerable institution.[113] After the First World War, a new community centre movement was to take off across the country, as a number of individuals, educational professionals and volunteers began to take to the idea. There was often local voluntary support for building community centres as memorials to the fallen in the First World War along with other initiatives. Famously, in Cambridgeshire, Henry Morris, the new Chief Education Officer of the county, had instituted the idea of 'community schools for everyone' from 1924. Used as schools for children during the day, the buildings and all facilities were available for community activities in the evening, another idea that had been promoted by Follett.[114] This movement spread to many parts of the country in one form or another, especially in the more rural counties of Oxfordshire, Hertfordshire, Somerset, Lincolnshire, Herefordshire and Monmouthshire, to name the early ones. They led the way in the idea of making community centres a modern reinterpretation of the traditional idea of village life.[115]

Cashmore was more interested in big cities and the often-large-scale new estates built on their peripheries. She saw them as marooned between the city centre and the rural areas and considered they were equally, if not more, in need of community building work, since the social base of the suburban estate was cut off from both city and countryside. It is not possible to plot the extent of her influence personally but at the end of the war she was becoming more influential in the settlement movement with her work towards creating a federation of residential settlements, which had gained considerable momentum. This made her in demand with other voluntary organisations seeking to readjust after the war, and she found herself discussing these 'community' issues in committees such as the Advisory Group of Voluntary Organisations and groups trying to form a National Council of Social Services.[116] She was invited to sit on the government's New Estates Committee, affiliated to its reconstruction programme and made up of representatives of settlements, educational groups and the National Council of Social Service.. Their remit was to look at the social issues that were emerging on new housing estates. This group reported to the committee chaired by Sir John Tudor Walters, charged by Lloyd George to consider the design and standards applied to new working-class housing in the post-war housing programme.

Garden suburb ideas took priority. On that committee was Raymond Unwin, architect of Letchworth Garden City and of Hampstead Garden Suburb, while Tudor Walters also held the post of chairman of the Hampstead Garden Suburb Trust. If town planners were giving physical form to the future, ensured by the post-war Tudor Walters standards, Cashmore was determined to highlight the social context. But she needed to be primed about the physical environment of the garden suburb. Accordingly, she set up a Bristol branch of the Garden Cities and Town Planning Association (GCTPA) and invited speakers to come and address the Public Utility Committee set up under the auspices of the National Spelter Works in Kings Weston. After the 1919 Town Planning Act, influenced by the findings of the Tudor Walters report, she wanted to start by making sure that Bristol built modern housing to the highest standards. She asked the national GCTPA how to set about putting pressure on the city council to ensure that everything was built to the very highest specifications.[117] She discovered that outside London, practical expertise on interior design was thin on the ground, with very little knowledge of the new developments conducive to helping women to run their households more easily and efficiently and which were flourishing at this time in Germany.[118] She lobbied Bristol Council hard and even before any social housing projects had been adopted, the Council agreed to set up a women's advisory committee. This had the following representatives: Mrs Falk from the Settlement; Mrs Burman of the Women's Co-operative Guild; a representative from the Social Service League and Miss Townsend in the chair. The committee worked hard for over two years, developing their ideas and collecting masses of data and information. Their report was at once substantial and detailed.

Its influence was negligible, however, due to the financial crisis of 1921 at the end of the post-war economic boom. Bristol Council decided not to build and shelved the report. Cashmore was furious. She organised a 'Housing Famine' campaign culminating in a huge meeting in the Colston Hall, with Alderman Sheppard in the chair, the Bishop of Kensington, chairman of the Kensington Housing Association and Margaret Bondfield as speakers.[119] However it was not until a couple of years later that Bristol began an era of building social housing. The first minority Labour Government, which took office in 1923, passed the Wheatley Housing Act in 1924, which set up more generous subsidies for cities and Bristol made a serious start on its programme.[120] Cashmore had learnt, though, the need to gain a national profile. Her work on the New Estates Committee to involve voluntary organisations in social work, had not only given her insights into housing and town planning, she was to take up promoting her idea of community centres ever more vigorously in the 1920s as she took on further responsibilities. Her work, alongside the developing National Council of Social Service, educational settlements and other bodies, was part of an integrated drive in the 1920s, in Sir Wyndham Deedes' words: "out of which the whole Community Centres movement has grown".[121]

Election as President of the Federation of Residential Settlements

1926 was a turning point in Hilda Cashmore's life: she had reached 50 and she could reflect on what she had achieved in Bristol and nationally and what she might do in the future. She had long been drawn to undertaking settlement work overseas and felt if she did not do it now, she would soon be too old. She wanted to take her settlement ideas to India, especially to a rural community that would face huge difficulties in the current fast changing economic and political conditions there. Her experience during the First World War in France and Poland had brought home to her the challenge that faced the rural poor in the twentieth century in the face of war, poverty and political change. The Quakers had 50 years previously set up a mission in a rural area of the United Provinces in India, in a place called Itarsi, a small market town on a busy railway junction. The mission was still working but had lost some of its momentum.[122] She wanted to go there and see if she could do something new, create a new educational settlement that could be put in touch with what was going on in other parts of the sub-continent. But she was faced with a dilemma. In 1926, her work for the Federation of Residential Settlements (FRS) had brought her to be considered for the top position of president of the organisation, the first woman and the first from a provincial settlement. Should she walk away?

In fact, just as she was trying to make a decision, another challenge arose for the settlement movement in the UK. Manchester University Settlement, the flagship of the English provincial settlements since its foundation in 1895, was on the verge of collapse. If she stayed in the UK and took up the presidency of FRS, would not the revival of the fortunes of Manchester be a top priority? She had been asked by JJ Mallon, Warden of Toynbee Hall and a strong supporter of Cashmore taking over as President, to suggest the name of someone who could save it. Cashmore tried hard with what turned out to be a fruitless search. She began to realise that if she cared about Manchester's survival, she might just have to take the job on herself. She knew how to do it and Manchester was still the kingpin of the provincial university settlements. Without it, the whole settlement movement would be weakened, possibly fatally. She did not want to do it—another grimy city centre district for a period of what she estimated would be four years, since it would take that long to turn around its fortunes. But if she did, she need not necessarily give up her plans for India. She would make her acceptance of the Manchester job subject to conditions.

These were twofold: first, a closer tie for the settlement with the University of Manchester, which was just contemplating introducing social science studies at this time, and so needing to find a means of offering students practical experience in social work. Secondly, she wanted to build a path to her exit so that, after she had completed the estimated 4 years of her wardenship (unfortunately for her it was to take her seven), she could finally get to India. For this, she saw that she would need an exploratory visit to India so that she could make realistic plans. Leaving the settlement would require the need for support there in her absence. She asked for the appointment of a co-warden, who would come initially part-time and then provide cover when she was ready to undertake her fact-finding leave and visit India. But she still had to respond to the invitation to take up the presidency of the Federation of Residential Settlements, which would run simultaneously with her time in Manchester. She decided to make a further condition of acceptance to the FRS Council that she would resign after three years. That was accepted and she took the post.

In 1926, when contemplating these commitments, she could reflect on the 22 years she had spent with her friend and colleague, Marian Pease, seven of them in the early days planning and thinking about settlement work, fifteen years making her ideas work in Bristol. Her success through emergencies and crises in the city had been phenomenal: through strikes, through the First World War, through the housing crisis and post-war unemployment. She had nurtured adult education in the city, drawing in many men who went on to hold positions in trade unions, in local government and in the labour movement. She had tried to engage with Bristol women well beyond her students. She had established strong contacts with the Women's Co-operative Guild and had thrown her weight into efforts to interest women in adult education. She had always put her energies into helping women, especially with their families and their chances of training for jobs outside the home, especially in the various branches of social work

Cashmore's experiences had shown that the changing circumstances of all citizens, not just the poor, were part of an ongoing evolutionary process: the hollowing out of the inner-city areas of industrial cities as urban peripheries developed, and as modern technologies transformed communications, manufacturing and the social and cultural life of the people. She wanted to work *with* the poor, not just *for* the poor, and with all citizens for that matter, especially women, in a democratic dialogue. She believed that setting up the Bristol University Settlement and her strenuous and committed labours for fifteen years had given her the experience and insight to see the possibilities of developing social work along more flexible and fruitful lines, responding to challenges as they happened in a particular city. Settlement workers learnt about them

BRISTOL GUILDSWOMEN WHO HAVE SERVED ON THE CENTRAL
COMMITTEE OR THE S.W. OR W. SECTION.

The Bristol Women's Co-operative Guild were strong supporters
of the University Settlement.

through direct practical experience and could collect information and data to inform the social policymaking of central government, bringing to the fore the importance of knowledge 'on the ground' and getting help for all where it was needed.

She wanted to take her vision to all settlements through her time as president. She saw this unique opportunity as the first woman and the first from the provinces to have a real voice in the movement. It was a chance to wake up the settlement movement as a whole to the challenges of modern society. But she had barely started her presidency when there was one of the greatest moments of national crisis in British labour history, the General Strike of May 1926. It unleashed a maelstrom of strong emotions that made her determined to tackle full-on the future of the settlement movement in the UK. She had already begun to do this, prompted by the prospect of the first international meeting of representatives of settlements from different countries in Paris in July 1926. Meanwhile, the annual meeting of the Federation of Residential Settlements was to take place in June and Cashmore wished to use it to gauge the opinions of those in the British movement and to try and weld them together so that she could present a united British front in Paris. A couple of months before the General Strike, she had held a meeting of the executive committee to plan the FRS annual conference prior to the Paris meeting in July.

At this meeting, Cashmore hoped to bring the representatives on the executive committee together to recognise and respond creatively to the realities of modern social life in cities. To this end, she threw out some key questions:

> Can bodies like our present Settlements, so various in origin, their tradition and their outlook, really have anything in common, however deeply you go down, anything that can truly be said to give them unity of purpose to make their members part of a conscious group with a living fellowship with one another? ...Will they ever be able to act together sufficiently to drive their points home in times of national difficulty?[123]

There was considerable disagreement on the committee about these issues and a resolution was made to take these differences to the FRS annual conference in June, where Cashmore would sum them up, give her own views and ask for feedback. Between these two meetings, the national strike took place. Cashmore was left with the task of giving her verdict on her colleagues' views in public at the FRS conference, in a social and political environment shaken to its roots, despite the fact that the strike ultimately failed. She did so with vigour. She was ready to hit her audience hard.

She summed up the answers she had had from her committee members under three headings: those who still clung to Barnett's view of the settlement as a bridge between the 'Two Nations'; those who were pessimistic about current social conflicts, describing the situation as being like a river in flood; and the third group who saw settlements as divided in two, diametrically opposed social and political terms: the people who were being 'helped' who were "working men and women as 'labour'—the other people, the worthy people at annual meetings and councils as 'conservatives'". She soundly rejected them all:

> I do not believe a bridge is of any use anymore: the floods are out. I do not agree that because the sea is raging that our work is futile. I believe that now is our opportunity. I do not regard the matter from a political standpoint. I do not mind what politics are represented at our council meetings, provided they all are. I believe that the Settlements now have their supreme opportunity if they can understand it and use it.[124]

She had decided to use evidence of what had happened at the Bristol University Settlement during the General Strike as grounds for optimism. She described at length the settlement meeting that had been held in Bristol at the beginning of the strike and who were present:

> Our Council met in the darkest days of the strike in the old Council Chamber of the University. A professor was in the Chair, next sat a University Lecturer, then the Vicar of the biggest parish in our district, then a Secretary of the Co-operative Women's Guild, then the wife of our Labour Councillor and Guardian, who is a representative of the Settlement Association in our neighbourhood, then another working woman, representing the WEA, then the cashier at a great Cold Storage near us, another representative of our neighbours, then a University Lecturer, a senior master in a great public school, a Professor of History, an Inspector of Schools,

a representative of the Students' Settlement Association at the University; another representative of Labour, representative of the Residents' Association of the Settlement, another master of the same public school, two members of Council connected with the management of great firms. All these almost without exception are actively engaged in Settlement activities and the main business was what action, if any, should be taken by the Settlement in the Strike.

All agreed to open the Settlement Halls at once to unemployed men and boys; to stop for a time any letting of hall for any political party whatever; to open Settlement House to women and girls out of work; to open a Canteen forthwith for women and young babies and young children who would suffer.

A Conservative offered money, a Liberal offered helpers, the working class representatives offered stewards and money and all agreed without question. They knew each other and only wished to make their contribution.

So in the neighbourhood, the response was immediate everywhere. No one seemed to suspect our motives and all respected our non-party position. A local branch of the Dockers' Union sent a message of appreciation. The Hall was full of men and lads. But this comes from the deliberate work of years. It is the result of friendship on a basis of equal sharing of the common experience of life in the neighbourhood, formed slowly in daily contact.[125]

What she saw in this was a demonstration of 'social citizenship' in action in a humane society: a force for the well-being of all citizens through any circumstances, even a crisis as politically divisive as a national strike. The role of a settlement in such situations was not to take sides. The people who suffered most were the women and children and there was a need to feed all members of families. In a city, all could share the recognition of how suffering for the cause was playing into the hands of the already rich and powerful. She believed in social justice, negotiating between warring sides, not using force, especially the force of starving people to submission like a besieged city in the Middle Ages.

She believed she had made it possible for the people of Bristol to take this stance since the non-political settlement had built up a rare trust between all sorts and conditions of people (hence her list of who was at the meeting). The settlement was a civic resource that stood apart from politics and class, that could see the suffering of the disadvantaged as a civic emergency, a disinterested party between politicians, capitalists and workers. It was also there to play a part in the process of modernising urban society, to ease the process and make sure all benefitted from it.

In her speech, she mentions directly the work of Mary Parker Follett, referring her audience to Follett's work, *The New State*, only recently published in the UK in 1918. In this book, Follett argues that society is not fragmented but made up of groups. The critical challenge was to connect those groups in local networks as this was the key to developing democratic advance. "The study of democracy" she wrote, "has been based largely on the study of institutions: it should be based on how men behave together".[126] Following Follett, Cashmore saw the settlement movement with its combination of support for education outside formal education, and concern for people and place across the city, as a central vehicle for connecting people across the divides of the particular 'groups' they belonged to. It could lead to making possible improvements in the quality of life of all citizens. It was an essential force in times of political emergencies. Cashmore was basically confronting her audience, those engaged in social welfare work, voluntary or professional, with the fundamental question: what is modern urban society and how is it possible to make it better?

Her contact with city expansion and new suburbs had focussed her mind on how this process, largely unplanned and directed by market forces, had contributed to a fragmentation of society, with attendant total lack of trust between different groups and a magnification of anger and outrage, as seen during the General Strike, when there was no chance of redress of social inequalities. She said:

It is no use blinking our eyes to the fact that we are building country house suburbs, motor fed, for our successful business men—garden suburbs, 'bus fed for our clerks and upper grade factory officials—tram fed areas for our slum population … it is … a picture laid out like a relief map 'raised letters for the blind' of the industrial hierarchy under which we all live... There are better material conditions in these new suburbs...

There is better air, a better chance... [but] the class tradition goes on, only intensified, while the tie of neighbourliness, 'all the life of the street' is weakened.

Surely the Settlement fellowships should be out there, first if possible, and should cooperate to build up on new lines a community life.

To press her point home Cashmore then used two visual aids that would make her ideas crystal clear and resonate hugely with her audience. The first (see Page 68) was the diagram of society that had been used as the frontispiece of every Charity Organisation Society training manual since the late nineteenth century, a textbook that had gone through many editions and that had been used by most of the audience of voluntary social workers present. This diagram was so well known that nothing about it was ever questioned. It seemed simply an obvious way of representing the importance of the personal characteristics of the individual and their own efforts to support themselves and help social workers to differentiate between the 'deserving' and the 'undeserving'. Cashmore wanted to use it to demonstrate to her audience that it was based on a totally fictitious idea of what society was like and how social workers should look at society.

She wanted her audience to look at the COS diagram critically. At its centre is the individual, though surrounded by their personal family. Key here are the personal qualities of that individual and their family life—necessary ones are listed as 'Affection, Training, Endeavour, Social Development—all revolving around self-discipline and respectability and ideas of self-help dear to Victorians who believed in progress. Beyond the family, if you were lucky, were more relatives and friends. Then the true nature of the sub-text (or image!) of the diagram becomes clear—every single stage that follows has, at its core, personal and social discipline. Neighbourhood forces include landlords, tradesmen, employers, clergymen, trade unions (which were in the 1870s, in the early days of the COS, dominated by the very respectable unions of the 'labour aristocracy') and self-help institutions (savings banks, building societies, libraries, educational clubs, classes, settlements—created in the Barnett model).

By the time the next category is reached, *Civic forces,* disciplinary forces have increased: schoolteachers, school attendance officers, police,

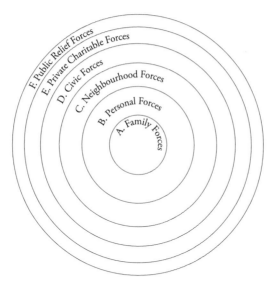

A.—FAMILY FORCES:
Capacity of each family member for Affection.
Training.
Endeavour.
Social Development.

B.—PERSONAL FORCES:
Relatives.
Friends.

C.—NEIGHBOURHOOD FORCES:
Neighbours, landlords, tradesmen.
Former and present employers.
Clergymen, Ministers, Sunday School teachers, fellow Church members.
Doctors
Trade-unions, fraternal and benefit societies, social clubs, fellow-workmen.
Libraries, educational clubs, classes, settlements.
Thrift agencies, savings-banks, stamp-savings, building societies.

D.—CIVIC FORCES:
School Teachers, attendance officers.
Police, magistrates, reformatories.
Health department, milk depot, sanitary inspectors, factory inspectors.
Disinfecting station, free disinfectants, whitewash and brushes (apply Town Hall).

Parks, baths.

E.—PRIVATE CHARITABLE FORCES:
Charity Organisation Society.
Church or denomination to which family belongs.
Benevolent individuals.
National, special, and general relief societies.
Charitable employment.
Cinderella club, children's summer holiday society, orphanages, day nurseries, society for protection of children.
District nurses, ladies' charity, hospitals convalescent homes.
Poor man's lawyer.
Discharge prisoners' aid society.

F.—PUBLIC RELIEF FORCES:
Relieving officer, district medical officer.
Poor Law Hospitals and sanatorium.
Fever and small-pox hospitals.

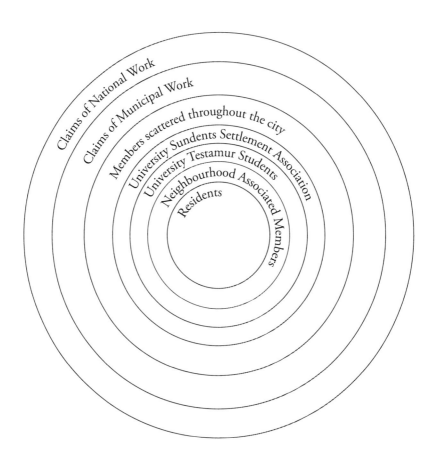

Claims of National Work
Claims of Municipal Work
Members scattered throughout the city
University Sundents Settlement Association
University Testamur Students
Neighbourhood Associated Members
Residents

Left—Diagram used as frontispiece in all texts on voluntary social work by the Charity Organisation Society. Social worthiness depended on individual character. Core of society: A-B personal; C-D social and civic; E philanthropic, F Emergency services for destitution and disease. There was no social dynamic. Since A-B was the social key, it allowed for E to work within the sifting process of the 'deserving' and the 'underserving' poor.

Above—Hilda Cashmore's alternative model, implanting democratic 'welfare systems' for health and happiness of the people in specific cities and regions as they changed and sending information up through government structures to inform national social policies.

magistrates and reformatories, sanitary inspectors, factory inspectors and so on. Then **Private charitable forces** headed by the COS who, of course, only gave any charitable assistance at all after careful casework and an interview, where the applicant is questioned by a panel of middle class volunteers about their circumstances and why they needed help.[127] Following this example, there was a range of specific charities—all of whom would also give only to the 'deserving'; and finally **Public relief forces**, the top being the relieving officer of the Poor Law who gave no relief whatsoever outside the workhouse (the law on this was tightened up in the 1890s) and did not discriminate between the 'deserving' and the 'undeserving', treating all in a sex-segregated harsh and highly disciplined system. There was no connecting link between these social services except what was assumed to be the continued personal failures of any applicant that actually passed through these various stages. In many ways it was a dismal view of how social services had evolved in a class society.

Clement Attlee, who was to become Prime Minister in the 1945 Labour government and oversee the passing of the welfare state legislation, had been a social worker at a Stepney boys' club for fourteen years and also briefly at Toynbee Hall. In 1920, six years before Cashmore's lecture, he wrote a book, *The Social Worker*, laying out his ideas on modern social work and what he hoped would be its possible future. He suggested:

> The Social Service movement of modern times is not confined to one class, nor is it the preserve of a particular section of dull and respectable people. It has arisen out of a deep discontent with society as at present constituted, and among its prophets have been the greatest spirits of our time. It is not a movement concerned alone with the material, with housing and drains, clinics and feeding centres, gas and water, but is the expression of social justice, for freedom and beauty, and for the better apportionment of all the things that make up a good life. It is the constructive side of the criticism passed by the reformer and revolutionary on the failure of our industrial society to provide a fit environment where a good life should be possible for all.[128]

This was definitely how Cashmore saw social services and the purpose of her lecture was to try and convince other settlement workers to take a critical look at the COS diagram the better to see new ways forward.

Cashmore then put her own diagram (see Page 69) alongside the COS version of society. The most important difference was her belief that what makes society are the relations between groups of people from all economic and social levels, not personal behaviours.[129] This was a perceptive point about modern society that has only become more noticeable in the twenty-first century where 'group' consciousness exists outside the political system, that has become more prone to pandering to the most vociferous opinions in an attempt to reap political advantage. Cashmore's view of groups in society is that they could be a force for good, campaigning for humanity and social justice. Notice the completely different infill of categories and interpretations in her version. She wanted to propose a dynamic model, aware of the shifting nature of urban populations and their circumstances. Her 'welfare' system is embedded in the city and region because she was aware from practical experience that the changing conditions of modern life, the conditions she had seen in the US: migration patterns, poverty, inadequate and poor-quality housing and unemployment, are experienced at the local and regional level in ways not necessarily encompassed by national policies.

State policy was very important in making national policies aimed at a basic minimum standard for all. But voluntary organisations had a wider remit and understanding of the effect that the process of 'modernisation' was having both on the people and the place, even combatting to some degree the degradation of the local physical environment.[130] As an optimist and believer in what could be done if people are in contact with each other, within and between their different groups and beyond the limits of a narrow political focus, she hoped this would make for a higher level of well-being for all in the twentieth century.

Cashmore believed that 'society' as a social construct exists, whatever form the built environment takes in an industrial society, and that it is made up of shifting groups.[131] In her paper she suggested there needs to be "constant action and interaction between these circles and groups" to make society cohesive, peaceful and flourishing. But to make a contribution to the life of the nation and to the city and its region, and to all its citizens, there has to be some way of bringing people together to coordinate work for the greater good. The title of her paper, *Settlements and Citizenship*, suggests her framework for this. On the one hand is the settlement, a voluntary civic organisation that "does cut through class distinctions, denominations, jealousies and industrial strife and actually does hold on its way and is strong enough to hold up its head as a Peacemaker." On the other hand, the settlement also has a wide reach, representing not only past and present residents but also the many other citizens and groups who choose to join the Settlement Association, which is open to all.

This was crucial for the work she saw the settlement doing. It worked for the people by articulating their desires and encourages collective action on municipal causes that benefit everyone. It can do this because the settlement's organisation shapes this work giving it a strong sense of direction. It also acts as a restraint in refusing to undertake the irrelevant. But its two final characteristics are the key ones. First, it produces "a group mind very sensitive to the undercurrents of feeling, very quick to interpret the inarticulate gropings of the mind of the people". By this she meant the settlement was really in touch with all citizens in the city and through experience and deep local knowledge could give voice to how people felt, what they wanted and needed. Secondly, it brought people together through connecting the representatives of all circles highlighted in Cashmore's diagram and made it possible to gather practical results which could be circulated to government, both local and national. It gives the city a voice and support to all citizens.[132]

She acknowledged the importance of the fact that the settlement was a university settlement since its regulating body supported the quality of the academic and practical work it undertook; and the university benefitted because the settlement fulfilled part of its remit as a modern provincial university. The University of Bristol could claim a double mission: on the one hand world-class scholarship, research and teaching; on the other, responsibility for the economic, social and cultural development of city and region. Key members of the settlement were her Testamur students, who had hands-on experience through their training in practical social work. This was the 'rock face' where the impact of social and economic change in the city could be seen and measured. The students cared and this helped considerably to create the 'red hot heat' at the 'centre' of Cashmore's diagram, together with those citizens of Bristol who were passionate about trying to bring about social change through the settlement Members' Association. The first group were vital for making sure that there would be strong responses to the next generation of social challenges and the latter provided the intensity of heat from the centre that could publicise the problems.[133] This heat would draw in individuals, circles and groups in common activities and policies.[134]

Finally, in the diagram's outer circles, the settlement could channel demands for more social services at municipal level and, beyond that, 'national work' to back up what had been achieved. This was, crucially, a way of creating the general well-being of society from below, based on an understanding of the challenges of a largely urbanised society. It could create a sense of a common humanity shared between social workers, politicians, philanthropists and the people.[135] It could build a society where people were in harmony with themselves and with their environment. Cashmore thought that if she could inspire all the settlements across the country to follow this path, it could make a real difference. They could unite on major national problems such as bringing to the top of the agenda the long-term unemployment of men and women that had decimated whole communities.[136] She counted this as a force, pointing out that there were 70 settlements and 26 educational settlements, "some 96 groups in this very small country".

These 96 groups could collect knowledge and experience of particular places, problems and possibilities as "at present much of it flows away with the stream of daily life". She asked at the conference for funding for a research worker who could collect all this evidence "for the purpose of driving home to Members of Parliament, government departments and central associations what we think and believe are the instruments we have." The voice of settlements had not reached parliament, but, in the period 1904–1919, ten universities had gained departments of social sciences and her views on society and new directions for social work were echoed in all of them. Her words at the FRS Conference had been passionate and her arguments strong but she did not carry the day. They were too radical for the audience. How was she to get her message across to all members of the settlements, not just those who attended the conference?

The settlements had had a voice in post-war reconstruction largely due to efforts she had made, but the voluntary sector as a whole had to some extent lost confidence in its direction, especially in relation to state provision of welfare. It took some time in the immediate post-war period for the National Council of Social Service to get recognized and established.[137] The rise of mass politics could only get stronger and be more polarized in the 1920s as post-war problems wreaked havoc on Britain's basic staple industries: coal, textiles, iron and steel and heavy engineering. At the same time the willingness of government to increase its commitment towards developing policies to ease social problems in the post-war period quickly declined from its war-time level when there had been a political incentive to pacify workers' discontents. Early failure of the 'Homes for Heroes' campaign that contributed to the 1919 election victory for Lloyd George ended up as a catalogue of mistakes caused mainly by two problems: civil servants in central government with little idea how to initiate mass housing programmes; and then local governments, unpractised in the practical logistics of getting large scale building projects off the ground.[138] But Cashmore was still willing to fight on. She was to put a great deal of energy into her period of office as President of the Federation of Residential Settlements. Her first coup was to get the name of the Federation changed to the British Association of Residential Settlements (BARS). This made it less like a club led and totally dominated by male wardens located in London. The female wardens of London's women's settlements who attended annual settlement meetings had never been allowed to hold any official office in the Federation, which makes Cashmore's elevation to the Presidency all the more remarkable.[139]

Cashmore was also ready to tackle head-on this tradition of the gender divide.[140] Minutes of an executive meeting in 1927, with Cashmore as chair, record: "that in her opinion the time had come to drop the expression "Men's Settlements" and "Women's Settlements" and speak of "Settlements" only...". The committee entirely agreed in this opinion.'[141] Cashmore also tried to break down the exclusivity of her settlement movement and to forge links with similar kinds of organisation such as the Educational Settlements Association (ESA), with a view to sharing local and regional resources where appropriate. But she found the Education Act of 1918 had put a barrier between them by funding the ESA and not the settlements. However, she had some success on the personal front by engaging the services of Sir Wyndham Deedes to serve on the BARS executive committee. He was to work for BARS in parallel with the work he was doing for the National Council of Social Service. Deedes was an extraordinary figure. He had a distinguished war that had led to a diplomatic role after 1918, due to his brilliant administrative skills and his talent for languages; already fluent in Dutch and German, he later became fluent in Turkish and Arabic.

The Settlement's flourishing football team.

His last assignment in the post-war period had been in the Middle East where he was tasked with the considerable diplomatic problem of making Arabs and Jews talk to each other, while working out complicated agreements.[142] Back in the UK, he rejected his family's stately homes in Kent and had gone to live, in 1923 and at the age of 40, in two rooms in University House Settlement in Bethnal Green, devoting himself thenceforth to voluntary social work. Deedes quickly recognised the importance of getting the settlement movement embedded and supported in the provinces if it was to have any impact on post-war society. He also recognised the importance of collecting information about the work of existing settlements, connecting them with each other and supporting their work. With Cashmore as president and Deedes as honorary secretary, BARS was to follow a radical programme. The executive committee consisted only of these two and the treasurer,[143] who had very little money to oversee and spent his time trying to raise funds. It meant that Cashmore and Deedes were able to get things moving.

They discussed strategies for trying to bring the settlement movement more closely together, concluding that the best idea was to visit the settlements one by one and make personal contacts while gathering data (the 'scientific' approach). Deedes volunteered to do this, and he continued with this work over a number of years, both for the Settlement Association and for the NCSS for whom he was also honorary secretary. Cashmore's big hope, though, was to expand the work she had done in Bristol and was doing in Manchester, trying to create the inclusion of social groups within all aspects of city life as the primary objective for the future, through community centres linked with settlements. She wanted to promote this across the country as new estates continued to appear on the peripheries of many cities, large and small.[144]

The government had even shown a little interest in the community centre movement by the mid-1920s. The militancy of the labour movement around the General Strike and the financial crisis of 1926, the problems of declining industries and unemployed workers, and the two combined in the case of the militant coal miners in the less profitable coalfields, demanded some action from the government. The coal industry in particular provided a very specific set of problems. The idea had been floated that, as the South Yorkshire pits became less economic, a solution may be to move the miners, lock stock and barrel, south to Kent, where there were coalfields not fully exploited. Kent County Council, aware of this possibility in their highly rural county, quickly commissioned Patrick Abercrombie, who had been trying, mostly unsuccessfully, to get local authorities to think of regional planning for their futures, to carry out a survey for a regional planning scheme. It was a highly politically sensitive project. The miners had a strong sense of community related to their pits and villages; the rural communities of Kent were alarmed at the introduction of coalpits and incomers. Abercrombie asked Cashmore for help on how to achieve a satisfactory social outcome. In fact, the whole project did not get very far. Abercrombie submitted his final Report in 1928 and the Wall Street crash the following year put an end to it.

However, Cashmore managed

Sir Wyndham Deedes.

to retrieve something from this. One or two small pits had been developed some years earlier and were operational. A small number of South Yorkshire miners were relocated to these, especially around Elvington, a small housing estate. Cashmore wanted to set up a Community Centre there with a trained warden who could militate against social frictions. The records of BARS are full of matters concerning Elvington Community Centre, notably the problems of financing and sustaining it. That had to be solved by setting up an independent company to hold any funds that could be raised since BARS notoriously did not have any funds itself. The critical factor though that made it work initially, was that she was able in 1930 to appoint a brilliant first warden, Mabel Phythian, whom she had met in Manchester. Unfortunately, she only stayed for two years, leaving to get married, an increasing hazard in the interwar years when recruiting female wardens for new community centres.[145] She left early on in Cashmore's time as president; the problem of finding the talented people who could take on this work magnified, especially as the size of the new estates also became much greater.

In the late 1920s, London County Council had begun building huge new housing estates, called 'cottage' estates to signify their rural context, at Becontree and Dagenham. The problems for the early tenants were huge. No thought was initially given to creating jobs, the idea being that trains could transport the male workers into the City. It was a simplistic vision. As for the lives of women and children, apart from building one or two schools and a few small shops, there was very little else. Women's lives were particularly adversely affected. Those moving to these estates were experiencing, in extreme form, the difference between living in an inner-city and life on a new estate a considerable distance from London, cut off from civic society and social support. There was much hand wringing by the BARS executive that these new estates were just too big for the Association. It was suggested rather hesitantly that the South London Settlement might make an attempt at developing some outposts there, but they needed institutional backing to handle administration and financial matters. Cashmore suggested the University of London, which was rather unlikely, but even more important for her was to find an enthusiastic trained individual to launch the scheme as the first warden and to make sure that the people themselves were democratically involved in the project. None of these things were forthcoming.

The scale was obviously beyond unfinanced voluntary effort. Cashmore managed to have more success with smaller ventures. It was a BARS initiative that resulted in the setting up of the settlement at Spennymoor in the depressed South West Durham Coalfield, funded by the Pilgrim Trust.[146] As BARS president she was also asked by her old friend, Violet Markham (for whom she had worked in her very first settlement job in Chesterfield), to appoint a new warden for the Woodlands Settlement at Doncaster that Markham had started and was willing to continue funding. She was successful in that. Cashmore herself also had some success in Manchester, launching community centres on two small-scale estates, the Wilbraham Road Estate Settlement, and the Newton Heath project, that she attached to the Manchester Settlement. She had done what she could in the three years that she had agreed to serve BARS, but she was never able to shift the 'traditionalist' approach to social work, especially amongst the male dominated settlements. As she had planned, she stepped down in 1929 from BARS. Her time as president had coincided with the hands-on, strenuous work of reviving the Manchester University Settlement. It must have been a heavy workload but at least in Manchester it was work she enjoyed and was best at—working in the midst of groups of people, forging personal contacts and inspiring enthusiastic young volunteers towards realising achievable goals.

Saving the Manchester University Settlement

Manchester greeted her with open arms when she finally got there in the autumn of 1926. She had come with the highest reputation and she did not disappoint. The two key figures who gave her the warmest welcome were Mary Stocks, herself a social worker, and her husband, John Stocks, a Professor of Philosophy at Manchester University. Both were ardent supporters of the university settlement. Mary was to write a history of the settlement in which she designated Cashmore's time as warden as "another Golden Age", matching long past achievements of a former deputy warden, Alice Crompton.[147] Cashmore and John Stocks were to work extremely well together on settlement business.[148] He had been trying to sustain the settlement since arriving in Manchester in 1924. They seemed to have only had one 'bone of contention'. He had tried very hard to raise funds from rich industrialists but when he got invitations to dine with them Cashmore resolutely refused to go. Her grounds were the way they treated their workers in terms of pay and conditions. But this potential conflict between John Stocks and Hilda, though commented on by Mary somewhat acerbically, was happily resolved by a chance: a huge bequest to the settlement.[149]

Working with Cashmore, Stocks took on several important roles. He became the 'University Liaison Officer', working on behalf of securing the essential connection between the settlement and the university that Cashmore wanted, with social science students coming to the settlement for training. Meanwhile Cashmore set about seizing the opportunity to reorganise the physical buildings of the settlement, now rather dilapidated, to make them serviceable for a new range of activities. Together they launched a bid for donations to achieve all this. They were extremely fortunate that, just at this moment, the settlement received the very large benefaction of more than £6,000 from the recently deceased Alice Bickham, a distant relative of TC Horsfall, the industrialist and passionate advocate of town planning, who had left much of his estate to her.[150] He had, of course, been closely associated with the settlement in the early days, offering it a base for its activities in Ancoats Hall which he had purchased to use for his Ruskinian art museum. He was also a passionate advocate of town planning,[151] setting up another tradition that Cashmore was to pursue.

The legacy was to make possible a dramatic reconstruction and rearrangement of the settlement site and buildings. The biggest change was to rescue the 1821 chapel behind the settlement buildings whose graveyard had already been purchased to provide for some open space for children's games and other activities. The old circular chapel with its classical windows was to become the centre of the settlement, its heartbeat and main attraction. When the builders started renovations, the floor, ceilings and roof of the building all collapsed, leaving only the outer walls. This was a great boon as the interior could be built from scratch. The emphasis of activities in the new Round House was on recreation and leisure and pleasure activities for all. This was a step change in Cashmore's settlement work.

In the early 1920s, she had recruited a young woman she met in London, a Quaker, Winifred Gill (1891–1981), who wanted to commit herself to social work. Cashmore invited her to Bristol and Gill became a resident at the settlement. She may not have had practical social work training (which Cashmore was very happy to provide) but she had many skills and talents, especially of the kind that Cashmore recognised would help in the modernisation of settlement activities.[152] She was to take Winifred with her to work in Manchester in 1926. The age gap between Gill and Cashmore was roughly the same as that between Cashmore and Marian Pease. Gill was the new generation, just as Cashmore had been in her time in Bristol. Gill had studied art at the Slade school in her teenage years but in her formative years, in her early 20s, she had become an assistant to Roger Fry (the art critic and artist, one of Marian Pease's cousins), who had set up the Omega Gallery and Workshops in Bloomsbury in 1913.[153] Fry discovered he was useless at management, especially running a thriving, successful and avant-garde business, such as the Omega Gallery, patronised by the Bloomsbury Group of writers, artists, poets and playwrights and even the economist JM Keynes. He had handed it all over to her, aged 23 and inexperienced, to manage.

Remarkably, Gill flourished. Fry then went off on a visit to France that included meeting his sister, Margery Fry, then working on the Marne in the same job and in the same organisation as Hilda Cashmore had done in 1914.[154] At the end of the war, Fry returned to London and closed the gallery. Gill decided that in her next venture she would like to become a social worker. She enjoyed working at the Bristol Settlement and with Hilda, so was very happy to go to Manchester in 1926. Winifred's work, first in Bristol and then in Manchester, was very popular. She painted the theatre sets for an expanding number of plays put on in the Manchester Round House and utilised her varied skills in the arts, handicrafts and drama, attracting many takers for her different classes. One of her Manchester classes was an established weekly class she took over of blind people. Hilda had arranged for her Bristol and Somerset friends to send fresh scented flowers to the class from their gardens every week, for their pleasure.

Winifred became so important, both in Bristol and Manchester, because her skills suited the major shift Cashmore had become aware of, towards prioritising leisure and pleasure activities at the settlement itself to sustain support from the local people and beyond. Even in Bristol, Cashmore had seen that some of the educational activities of the settlement were now being taken over by newer institutions such as the Folk House, a joint venture between the former Baptist Mission and the Bristol Adult School Union in 1920. It was affiliated to the Educational Settlements Association, also established in 1920. Its great advantages were that it was located in the city centre within easy reach of potential students from all over the city; it could also offer a very wide range of education and cultural activities and it attracted large numbers of both young men and, importantly, young women too.[155] The 'golden era' of the Workers' Educational Association was before the First World War, when mostly working men came for classes in a serious bid for personal self-improvement. Now leisure, fun, sociability *and* educational classes in an informal setting were what drew the students.

Hilda was ready to embrace these changes in Manchester and was able to do so, as gradually, over the next couple of years, the reconstruction of the old chapel took form and became the Round House, the centre for settlement activities. Hilda herself got a great deal of personal enjoyment out of the burgeoning theatre programme in the Round House. She adored putting on plays and was an excellent producer. She was to cajole both WG Farrell, warden of Spennymoor Settlement, Durham, to come and give expert advice[156] and John Stocks to do some acting! This Professor of Philosophy was given a part in a production of *The Lady with the Lamp* in which he played the role of Palmerston. In a story told by Farrell, in the midst of rehearsal, everything came to a stop whilst Farrell and Stocks discussed how actors should move and use gesture on stage. Farrell admitted this discussion pleased him, but the point of his story is that it also pleased,

Miss Cashmore for she used to hover about listening-in and joining in the discussion with her eyes dancing *impishly* with glee. She did enjoy those days and moments … such a blend of youthful enjoyment and adult knowledge … it illuminates everything in its neighbourhood …[157]

Before the Roundhouse creation had been fully completed in 1928, however, Cashmore had managed, with the help of John Stocks, to get the position of Director of Practical Training for Social Work in connection with a projected diploma in social studies at Manchester University. It meant once again that Cashmore was in touch with students, and enthusiasm amongst students was such that requests from them to stay at the settlement outran the supply of accommodation. The kind of practical work that Cashmore was introducing to her Manchester students differed in a number of respects from her teaching in Bristol. She was aware, from the moment she had arrived in Manchester, that the city was changing fast, even the dismal neighbourhood of Ancoats. Slum clearance was underway, and the city was building new estates on the periphery. One of the subsidiary reasons that had helped her choice to come to Manchester was its housing policies and programme. She saw this as an opportunity to undertake the work of community building that she had started in Bristol on the new estates. Manchester of course had many more estates and there were plans for one of the largest in the UK in Wythenshawe.

The person behind this latter project was Sir Ernest Simon (1879–1960), a rich industrialist and director of a family engineering firm, whom Cashmore got to know well during his many visits to the settlement, when he discussed aspects of estate building and management and their social implications with her over dinner. Simon, later to be Lord Simon of Wythenshawe in 1947, had joined Manchester City Council in 1912, becoming a prominent member and, at the time, at age 42, the youngest ever Lord Mayor of Manchester in 1921–22. The Wythenshawe area had been identified in the early 1920s by the architect planner Patrick Abercrombie as the best site for developing a 'garden city' style estate. He had taken the commission because he was trying to promote urban planning of the city and region as a whole, as an essential means of securing the best future for all. When Cashmore went to Manchester in 1926, the Council had just published its first plan of the city and its region. In that year too, Simon personally purchased Wythenshawe Hall and park and donated it to the city. From then onwards, he took a keen interest in the planning of the largest future district in Manchester, the Wythenshawe estate.

But things went slowly. Simon became Liberal MP for Manchester Withington from 1923–4 and 1929–31, both periods when Parliament passed legislation promoting social housing. He was appointed Parliamentary Secretary to the Ministry of Health in August 1931, just after the passing of the Greenwood Housing Act of 1930 that focussed on slum clearance and rehousing schemes. While some building in small areas was begun in the 1920s, the project as a whole still did not get government go-ahead in full until after the Second World War. Simon and Cashmore continued their many discussions, both aware of their mutual passionate commitment to creating new ways for citizens to live in modern cities. They came to the matter, though, from clearly different standpoints—he, both from a government perspective and his experience in business wanting to get it planned and built; she, from the position of prospective tenants and giving a voice to the people whose lives were being so drastically changed and keeping them connected to the city where they had lived.

She recognized the importance of getting new social housing built in pleasant and healthy surroundings. But she was just as concerned about practical matters in the present and future: the huge number of people who needed some kind of social services to make life possible even before thinking about making it enjoyable. She argued that social contacts, jobs, local services and leisure pursuits mattered for young and old. As for women, in their former lives in city centre locations, even in slum housing, some mothers, and more often their daughters, could find employment. Women needed local support networks to find work and to deal with all the vicissitudes of working-class life. Society as they knew it had been taken away and there was no model for the future in peripheral housing estates. Simon listened but his interest was in the physical plan and the civil engineering of a huge council estate. This difference between Cashmore and Simon was an important one, as it was to mirror the fate of voluntary social services in the 1930s and 40s and beyond. 'Building the better Britain', ushered in the 'golden age' of state planning during and after the Second World War and it took precedence over 'building the better society'.

This blind spot in the modern British planning movement was caused basically by a lack of knowledge about urban working-class life that had spawned volunteer projects like Mass Observation, trying to learn about city life by looking at it; and GDH Cole's mega survey, begun in 1942, of British life, collecting data on everything, that eventually spun massively out of control by the end of the war.[158] Studies of Wythenshawe, itself mainly created in the post-Second World War era, have underlined the difficulties of living on the estate in the early days, especially for women.[159] Cashmore wanted to suggest that settlements had the experience and information that was much more pertinent to life in the 1940s (in fact many settlements including Bristol gathered information for Cole's Report). She really wanted to create a climate in which government would consider essential social policies and could take appropriate actions in different city contexts. She was hoping for a cross party consensus that the purpose of government social policy was to ensure the well-being of the people.

But in the 1920s and 30s, politics and ideology had sustained the class war in Britain. At least Simon and Manchester City Council were building new homes and producing plans for the future. But even that provoked strong opposition. Prospective city and regional planners were confronted with hostility to their work in political terms, 'planning' belonging to totalitarian regimes and being seen as an example of communism. Voluntary organisations in Britain were seen as the 'democratic' alternative to an authoritarian state system, but by the 1920s, their voluntary nature had become compromised as the links between the state and the voluntary sector had grown. The National Council of Social Service had tried and failed to broker a non-political relationship between the voluntary sector and government while sustaining support for regional centres and their voluntary organisations.[160] The key problem with 'planning' and government social policy was a very basic one: the political commitment of government. In the 20s and 30s, these political divisions intensified and ruled out any kind of consensus.

Cashmore was also aware that while the numbers of student volunteers wanting to help with social issues was still strong and growing, they, and the universities where they studied, were not so committed to the local context of the city, which had become less frequently the place where they had been brought up.[161] Their objectives were just different. Many university students got involved with the unemployed, offering summer vacations with activities. Recently graduated students looked abroad, such as the young doctors and nurses leaving for India and Africa to try and eradicate leprosy, and caring for the victims through the voluntary organisation, the British Empire Leprosy Relief Association. The vitality of a settlement depended on the next generation having a continuing commitment to engage with the local issues of their city and region and a democratic ideal of a shared way of life. It needed to include not just social services but also recreation and pleasure in local activities, from sport, to culture, to every kind of activity which was pleasurable to engage in communally. The settlement was still important but there was competition from good causes demanding attention for voluntary effort in the wider world and its many problems.

As she continued with her task of reviving Manchester (taking longer than she had hoped) Cashmore began to think ever more longingly about her desire to go and work in India. It had been a lifetime's ambition, probably as far back as her student days. Georgina Brewis' study, *A social history of student volunteering: Britain and beyond*, demonstrates how voluntary service abroad had begun to mushroom in the early years of the century amongst students and young people, especially for work in India. Cashmore had great sympathy with the young people now going to parts of the British Empire, especially India, not as missionaries, but to offer expertise and help, medical, educational and social services. Those people and countries faced a future not only of economic and social change, but also political struggle for independence, likely to change the lives of all.[162] She had already tried to make BARS recognise a changing world in the UK. She had also succeeded in reviving Manchester University Settlement and setting it on a new course, trying to connect the city centre with the new estates as they developed. She felt she had done her best to promote the community centre idea across the country and now the Council of Voluntary Social Service was taking it up and was making government listen. It had become a vigorous movement that remained strong from the late 1920s to the 1960s across Britain and, in a less centrally organised way, to the present day.[163] However, by the early 1930s, Cashmore's eyes were on India.

4. India: Cashmore's last project

Educational work in India in the 1930s

What Hilda Cashmore achieved in the last assignment in her career—her time in India from 1933–38—was to be remarkable. It is unsurprising that Marian Pease, who received a constant supply of letters from Hilda about her adventures, was so impressed that she devoted more than half of the Memorial Volume to this last major project, quoting at length from her letters. What Cashmore had set her sights on, as she explained to the Friends Service Council, was an educational settlement in the countryside:

> to which educated young Indians and English people from different parts of the country who are interested in new social problems could freely come to study, for meditation, for thinking. It should welcome those who wish to stay and study or to help for a period, or drop in and talk, or to come for a weekend or a summer school.[164]

The 'help' she would need related to an ancillary objective of organising social services for the Gond people who lived in villages within the great jungle (now a national park) in what were the British United Provinces. She felt she could set up these projects because there was already a Quaker foundation in Itarsi, only 12 miles from the jungle, where the Quakers in the nineteenth century had set up a religious mission, though engaged now with economic and social projects. She could start her search for suitable sites while initially staying there.

She hoped to unite the educational and social service functions in a new purpose-built settlement located, if possible, actually in the jungle. It was important for her that there was a practical element in her project and working in the Gonds' villages would be that—part of the daily routine of settlement life. She wanted to make contact with the Gonds, locked out by their poverty and caste from any support, even rudimentary health care, and for whom education was totally out of reach. The plight and future of the inhabitants of India's 75,000 villages, possibly influenced by what she had read of Gandhi's work, seemed to her both the most urgent of all and within her means to address, even if on this very small scale. What drove her to undertake this strenuous and possibly dangerous project in a remote country area? She felt that it was a duty and a privilege to be able to do whatever she could, personally, for India and Indians in this critical moment of their history. Indian men and women had to prepare themselves for their independent future in what was now the hostile environment of a British government, raging against challenges to the well-established administration of the British Raj.

As a pacifist, Cashmore was deeply impressed by Gandhi's stance. She believed, like her Quaker Friends, that what was needed were people on both sides, British and Indian, who would summon up enough trust to make possible negotiations that could bring the conflict to a peaceful end, including the withdrawal of the British from India. That challenge, and her direct experiences in the First World War in France and Poland witnessing the sufferings of the non-combatants when violence erupts, made her really want the Indian movement to succeed peacefully. She was always modest about what she could achieve, but as Pease wrote: 'she longed to do her part, however small, in the work of reconciliation'.[165] Cashmore was ready to offer her services, especially in education and social work, because she knew that she could use her long experience of reaching out to people, offering education to students at every level, giving the kind of education that was possibly needed most, in these very troubled days of the 1930s.

All those who knew her well understood where she was coming from with this desire. Her former colleague in BARS, William Deedes, was sensitive to, and deeply admiring of, the moral imperatives that he knew had driven her selfless actions. He was the only man amongst the contributors in the Memorial Volume. The comments he made there about Hilda's character were a eulogy on the qualities she had brought to her vocation. Having praised her *joie de vivre*, cheerfulness, humour and care for others, he also emphasized her amazing courage: "Hilda Cashmore was one of those people whom you would wish to have with you if you knew you were going to be in a 'tight place'". It was the greatest accolade an ex-army man and high-level diplomatic negotiator could give. It was also the characteristic that was to stand her in good stead in India. His final comment, however, was that the most impressive thing about her was her religion:

No-one could be in any doubt as to where her strength lay or what was the source of her grace and goodness. Can one say more about a person than that one is richer for having known them?[166]

She was also a brilliant organiser and was meticulous in her preparations. When she resigned from BARS in 1929, she continued to go to London from Manchester regularly, but now to the Friends Service Council which hosted the meetings she attended of the India Reconciliation Group. Her first objective was to be as fully informed as she could be on the social and political conditions in India at this time. These meetings not only helped with this, but also brought her personal contacts, and the Friends Service Council was the support body of Quaker social service initiatives that was to give her the crucial financial assistance to make her plans a reality. Top of the agenda for discussion at this time in Quaker meetings was the mass movement led by Gandhi. He was the first revolutionary in the world in the twentieth century to disavow violence to achieve his objectives, something that really appealed to the Quakers with their long history of pacifism. Gandhi had begun his civil disobedience movement in South Africa before the First World War but on his return to India in 1914 he launched the long-drawn-out struggle to free India using his revolutionary technique of 'satyagraha' (a combination of two Gujarati words *Truth* and *Force*) in the course of the 1920s.[167] By the early 1930s, he was wrong-footing the British civil servants in India by turning against them their own political theories and their own moral code of honourable behaviour.

Cashmore was convinced that this was the moment she must go to India, in the wake of one of the greatest achievements of Gandhi, the apex of his long apprenticeship in the use of the technique of *satyagraha*. This was the *salt satyagraha* of 1930. Nominally at issue was the hated tax on salt. The practice of taxing salt was a patently unfair one that the British had continued from earlier times, because it provided a lucrative source of income. It was not only unjust, but the level of the salt tax varied between states across India, and British controlled states kept putting the tariff up. Gandhi had organised a walk from his ashram near Ahmedabad to the Arabian Sea coast. He went with 79 followers and it was to take them 24 days to cover the 241 miles, but over the days of the journey, thousands joined in. On arrival at the coast at Dandi, he ceremonially broke the law by picking up grains of salt from the beach. By this time, not only India but the whole world was agog at this venture and what would ensue. It was a direct confrontation to British authority but without a shot fired. The Government was frightened and angry, and nearly 60,000 arrests were made, including of Gandhi himself. He was later released so he could negotiate a resolution with the Viceroy and the tax was abolished. It was the strongest show of strength so far by the Indians, and greatly encouraged the campaigners for independence.

In Manchester, Cashmore immediately asked for action on one of the pre-conditions she had made on taking the role of warden: when she had decided to leave, she wanted a co-warden for a period of transition to ensure that Manchester could be left on a sound footing and she herself could make proper plans for going, including taking a period of leave as soon as possible for a fact finding visit to India. She found an extremely able person prepared to take on the short-term role as co-warden, Lady Mabel Smith, a Yorkshire woman, an educationalist and supporter of Labour. By early January 1932, Cashmore was on the ship to India, for eight weeks leave, on her fact-finding mission, with two companions from the Friends Reconciliation Committee. They went straight to Itarsi, where the Quakers still had a presence (they were to make two visits there during their trip). From there, they spent a hectic time criss-crossing the country, especially the large cities connected by rail: Bombay, Delhi, Calcutta on the East-West mainline and several more on the North-South trunk line too. They were able to do this because Itarsi was a railway town that had grown on a junction between these two main routes, which was why it had been chosen in the first place for a Quaker Mission in the mid-nineteenth century, when the railways were being built.

Cashmore had been warmly welcomed and saw at first-hand how the Itarsi mission had been transformed from its nineteenth century form and now contained a hospital, a school, farming experiments, an industrial village and other work. She was also taken on trips in the surrounding countryside and saw the nearby jungle and the beautiful countryside around it. Cashmore was both captivated by the latter and clear now that her plan for a new settlement was possible. It would need a lot of energy and hard work, and she also needed to secure the promised funding from the Quakers. She returned to England, to report to the Friends Service Council and to withdraw from Manchester. By 1933, she was ready, and she gave in her notice at Manchester. The Friends Service Council had authorised ample funding for a settlement that even included a personal car for her, in recognition of the practical difficulties she would face in travelling beyond the railway. They also organised and paid for a number of young women volunteers, to go out sequentially, one by one, to help Hilda. Most of them had belonged to the committees she attended, and she knew them personally. She was to find their help vital on many occasions.

The first of these was Dorothy Hersey and she got swept away by Cashmore's enthusiasm and excitement at being in India at last. Hilda and Dorothy left London on 12th Oct 1934 and arrived in Itarsi 26 days later. Just nine days after their arrival, having given themselves little time to acclimatize, on impulse they joined the camp of a British male missionary and social worker and his three Indian companions. The men were just going off to the jungle for a fortnight's camping, to tour villages, offering "simple Adult School teaching and partly definite Gospel teaching". This would be her first experience of villages and their people. It was also her first experience of camping in India and walking through the jungle. She loved all of it. Cashmore was able to use her car, that she had named Prudence, for the first time as well, to carry their equipment.[168] She was then to spend those early weeks travelling to Nagpur and other places within easy reach from Itarsi by road and extending her contacts with educationalists and social workers in the vicinity and, most importantly to her, beginning her search for a site for her settlement. Two events sustained her excitement at being in India. The first was a visit to Gandhiji's ashram, near Wardha, where she stayed in the women's compound. Gandhi was out of prison and in residence. He invited her to accompany him on his "very rapid hour's walk both morning and evening", and she had "very useful discussions with him about her plans".[169] The second event was the All Indian Women's Conference in December 1934 in Karachi. She was delighted by the sight of the large numbers of women delegates going to the opening ceremony "all in their party saris-exquisite colours and embroideries and some beautiful faces-as they swept up the steps into the hall".[170]

What heartened her, though, was that the conference offered the sight of English and Indians collaborating in support for women and social reform. For the first time, two English women had been invited to give addresses, Maude Royden and Mrs Corbett Ashby, both prominent in the women's suffrage movement and social reforms in England. Cashmore was the same age as Maude Royden, who had also attended Cheltenham Ladies College, but she did not make personal contact—she always shunned any action that might lead to personal publicity. But her reputation had preceded her, and she was invited to go south to the hill station of Ootacamund in the hot season of 1935 and take part in the many educational events there. Apart from giving talks, Hilda was engaged to give three lecture courses on:

1. The School as a Community Centre;
2. Principles of Educational Social Service at School;
3. Can the School be a Centre for the whole neighbourhood?[171]

This division of subjects reflects the kind of courses she had given in England and she was anxious to know how the students, many of them senior people, felt about her approach.

Determined to find out, she took a remarkable step. She asked if the students might be divided and whether she could have the senior ones for a discussion. These included Indian heads of institutions, an Indian Professor of Psychology and his wife, a German couple (Jewish Christians turned out of Germany) and one Hindu solicitor:

> Well, they went ahead and expressed themselves very freely. They all agreed they wanted a certain fusion of Eastern and Western, but they hated and feared our mentality, our Ford's factories, our terrible religious *organisation,* the missionary attitude of superiority, our hurry and speed, our attention to the clock and the next meal in the midst of a most vital discussion, and so on. It was all most illuminating. They were amusing, but the iron had entered their soul.[172]

What Cashmore took from this always remained with her. But she understood that their hostility was not directed towards her or her work. One of them, Professor Manakam "came up to me and said it had been the best hour of the Conference and they could have all gone on for hours".[173] She felt that the space of the summer school had given a chance for Indian and English to meet equally, with benefit to both. It confirmed to her that the way she had worked in England was valid, always providing she adapted quite radically and was sensitive to cultural differences. There was a demand for education of all kinds and for social services constructed from the bottom up, concentrating on the social and physical health of the poorest where there was huge need. Settlement work gave all a chance to have some voice in their future, leaving pure politics, like Gandhi did, to others.

The settlement in Uttar Pradesh and the forest ashram for the Gond people

She returned to Itarsi in July 1935 and was to throw herself into non-stop work with passion and commitment, not taking a break (and that meant working every single day) for the next nine months. She had planned from the start that she would stay for three years and she wanted to establish her settlement, if possible, so firmly that it would bring lasting benefit to the neighbourhood it served. In fact, on her return to Itarsi, she was met immediately by two serious setbacks. Her next assistant for the period October 1935 to March 1936, Katherine Lloyd, was ill and unable to come. The second blow was even stronger. She had found a really beautiful site in the jungle for her settlement but could not persuade the Mulguzar (the overlord landlord) to sell her the land. He had five brothers with a share in this land and they unanimously refused to sell. "He would not have a Christian on his land for anything in the world—the villages would become Christian!"[174] Undaunted she continued to search and found an almost equally beautiful site close by, but this time owned by a more friendly Mulguzar, an old Hindu, and she got the British District Commissioner to help with negotiations. Whilst these were ongoing, Cashmore had, at last, some luck: a replacement for Miss Lloyd had been found, Ermyntrude Malet, who could come immediately. The next piece of luck was a surprise. She had begun to realise that it would take time to get a settlement built from scratch and she discovered that that there was already a set of buildings that had been run by the Quakers at Rasulia, barely more than a large village, ten miles from Itarsi and just one and a half miles from the jungle.

This complex of buildings was quite extensive and had been used as a school, an adult education centre and a holiday camp for Boy Scouts and other social groups. All these activities had collapsed during the First World War and the buildings had been vacant subsequently for twenty years. In India, vegetation and animal life take over very quickly, and the whole site appeared very derelict. But what Hilda saw was the opportunity to begin her social work at once if she could make these buildings work as a settlement. Ever practical, she saw there was no cost for land and buildings since the Quakers already owned them and she could get teams of workers to clean up the site and repair the buildings quite cheaply. The site was not beautiful, though it was set around by some beautiful trees. Importantly, the scale of the buildings was considerable, with one of the rooms being 100ft long, suitable for housing meetings and conferences of relatively large numbers, with access for participants via the railway. This would provide income to keep her settlement going. In no time at all, she had turned the site into a hive of activity, renovating the main bungalow as a residential facility, together with some cottages and other buildings for meetings and workshops. It was strenuous for her as nothing got done unless she attended to every detail personally. She travelled each day between Rasulia and Itarsi.

Soon after she had started this work at Rasulia, the alternative jungle site became available in Jamai. By now she decided that Rasulia could be the main Settlement and host large gatherings. At the jungle site she would build an 'ashram', a settlement outpost to be used for small meetings, discussions, meditations for educated young people seeking to study in a quiet place; and it could also act as an outpost, a base closer to the villages for developing social services for the Gond people. She had spotted a crucial way of reaching out to the people. The site was not far from a brickworks and she would need a great number of bricks for the main building at the ashram and the surrounding cottages. There were 200–300 labourers working at the brickworks, men, women and their children. These people and their families would welcome medical services and social support. Her settlement mission would be complete if she could direct social services to them. She needed to move quickly to get Rasulia operational and she decided to move from Itarsi and to live on site. She chose for herself an existing little hut that she jokes about in her letter to Marian Pease:

My little hut—I can just see you looking at it—isn't really half bad. It has one long narrow dark room and a nice square room and a go-down (a store-room) and a place for a bathroom [likely to have no sanitation and be equipped only with a bucket of water for washing]. It is entirely primitive and will have a lepped floor which means earth polished with cow dung … I am so thankful it is there: if I had had to live in the big bungalow in the midst of all this poverty, I should have been sick with shame.[175]

Once she was in residence, she had to hire staff: cook, waterman, gardener and sweeper. She also hired an ayah who was looking after a

Cashmore (second from right) in 1936 at her
forest settlement, Jamai Ashram.

little Indian girl orphan, Sumati, adopted at birth by a former missionary,
Mary Allen, a social worker who was to work at the ashram once it was
built. Mary Allen had just left for some furlough in Britain, so Cashmore
hired the same ayah and was rewarded by a big hug from Sumati, who
clung to her legs. Hilda was delighted and continued where possible to
collect children, writing that Sumati "would grow up as a Settlement
child for a bit".[176] Cashmore gives a graphic description of the Rasulia
buildings as they re-emerged as a habitable environment:

> I have about 26 working here: (1) women keeping the cattle
> who are eating up the fresh long grass; (2) women weeding
> pestilential weed over all the compound which breeds
> mosquitos. The Government gives notice when it is to be
> destroyed, then the villages drum round warning people; (3)
> Chamars (workers in stone) doing repairs to my little house;
> (4) Six more chamars lepping (polishing with cow dung) the
> great floor of the barn (large room) to make it tidy for Yearly

Meeting. It has not been done for 20 years. (5) bamboo basket workers, a caste to themselves, making a bamboo hedge to keep the goats out…. And so forth".[177]

There was no contractor, so Hilda had to project manage it, directing each worker personally herself. Ermyntrude Malet proved to be a great support when she arrived in October, not only with all the work going on but also as a personal friend; having her there cheered Hilda up immensely in the five months of her stay.

By November Cashmore was holding the first students' Summer School at Rasulia: 24 students and their professors from Hislop College, Nagpur; more from Indore College; and three more from the Agricultural College in Nagpur. Rasulia was ready just in the nick of time. Very soon there were many more visitors, as Diwali and Christmas were both celebrated and people arrived continuously, some announced, some not. Cashmore's little domestic team were sometimes stretched to their limits, especially the cook. At critical points both at Diwali and Christmas, Cashmore said she was saved by what she called two comically 'miraculous' events. On the first occasion, a complete stranger came to dinner and asked if she might leave her immaculate bearer and big car for ten days, thus providing labour and transport to get urgent supplies from Itarsi. At Christmas, actually Christmas Day, 15 unexpected visitors had eaten all the food[178], leaving Hilda and the core residents at the Settlement with nothing, when a tonga[179] arrived with an Indian teacher from the High School who had brought as a gift "a complete, beautifully cooked Indian dinner for five!"[180] While all this was happening, the future possibilities of the ashram in Jamai were being finalised. Ermyntrude then demonstrated her talents not only by singing beautifully during the Christmas festivities but also by drawing up a plan for the main building and layout of the cottages at Jamai. In January Cashmore also made contact with the owner of the brickworks and with the help of a close friend of his, a young Brahmin whom she had coached in his economic and history studies, she managed to obtain a supply of cheap bricks and the promise of support for her social work at the brickworks. Already she was hoping and thinking of setting up a mothers' and children's school, a dispensary and some education for the Gond children.

Hilda's letters to Marian give an indication of how quickly she was able to make things happen, largely by taking on more and more work herself. Soon there was a rapidly growing number of people coming to Rasulia from far and wide. Gradually everything was taking shape, including the organised plans for daily and weekly activities and the monthly and yearly meetings appropriate for a Quaker settlement. She was particularly pleased when many villagers turned up for the Monthly Meeting, not to be converted, but just to sit in a quiet place and feel that they belonged. Progress was even made on the forest ashram. In February 1936 the most critical action was completed: digging the well for water—which was thankfully found. In the wealth of details of vital actions and comings and goings in Rasulia, and now Jamai, three reasons stand out that explain Hilda's success while living in what seems a constant chaotic whirl. The first was how she would set the ball rolling on some practical objective and somehow, even in this remote part of UP, find competent people to take over from her. A very important factor here was the support she got from other Quakers and former missionaries. The second was her familiarity with settlement work, which gave her great personal flexibility and clear objectives. The third came towards the end of her time in India when she began serious work on the village uplift programmes being set up by the government of UP.

The key factor though, was her brilliant ability to connect with people. As Jamai progressed, she had the plans for the settlement and surrounding cottages drawn up by Ermyntrude, her assistant, who even supplied sketches for the workers of what the elevations would look like. Ermyn, as Hilda called her, had to return to London at the end of February and Hilda was left for a while on her own. Thus, when building began, she had to direct it herself. She walked daily through the forest from Rasulia to Jamai with her little dog Pat, which she enjoyed, not only because she liked dogs, but he was also some protection for her against the snakes that often crossed the path. But it was not easy work. By the end of March 1936, yet again she managed to make contact with a person who could help her. This was Ronald Priestman, a Quaker and social worker. He and his wife turned up at Rasulia to deliver books for Hilda's cherished library, gifts from Kathleen Lloyd the assistant who had been sick and replaced by Ermyn. Cashmore discovered he was an excellent builder and when she told him her predicament at Jamai, he "leapt at the suggestion that he should help".[181]

Another example of her ability to attract people and spot their talents was her concern about who should replace her when she finally left. She had determined she was leaving in three years. It had been her greatest worry since her arrival. With the huge effort she made in 1935 to get Rasulia functional again, with an ever-greater number of summer schools and meetings and a large gathering at Christmas, many people were coming to the settlement. At Christmas, her guests included people from the north and south of India: Elizabeth Booth, a Quaker, from Santiniketan, Rabindranath Tagore's National University in West Bengal; others from St Stephens College (where CF Andrews[182] had worked prior to his later career in education and social reform); three more English people and three Indians. One of the Indians who turned up was Mr Chetsingh from Katar, a well-known educationalist. He and his wife, who was a former lecturer in Madras Christian College, were obviously very interested by the settlement. Mr Chetsingh was to visit Rasulia again in August 1936, when the ashram was more developed. Hilda took him with her when she went to the brickworks at Jamai to negotiate future relations between the works and the ashram. The matter at hand was now not bricks, which had all been purchased, but Hilda's desire to reach the brick workers and their families and to set up a dispensary for them and other villagers.

When Hilda and Mr Chetsingh turned up at the brickworks, they were met very formally:

The event of my week was a most prosperous interview with the owner of the brickworks about which I have told you so much. R. Chetsingh and I went together on Monday—a truly interesting event. The little courtyard was alive at our approach and we were ushered into the office on the right. There sat, on the left, crossed-legged on white cotton cloth, the older son-in-law, the manager. The Diwan [local official] and two others, and another son-in-law arrived. He said that he admired Christians and that he did not see any difference at all between religions. Then in the middle, two chairs were placed for R.C.S. and me, and a little table in front of us, and opposite, the owner of the brickyards. He told us to address him and looked very severe. However, the ice broke and I found he was wholeheartedly desirous to give me access and to help in every possible way. I could come at 8.a.m. every morning for dressings, etc., have a dispensary and doctor every week in the afternoon. He would make a temporary out-patients department, give me a proper cupboard for the medicines, allow a foreman and a woman to come each day so as to learn a little, too![183]

Hilda agreed readily, taking on another onerous and time-consuming role, but for her there was the greater prize: she had demonstrated the importance of the work to Mr Chetsingh, and he and his wife agreed to take over the settlement on her departure, which she thought would be in about a year's time. She felt she had managed to recruit not one warden but two.

Meanwhile, inevitably, she found her morning visits too much and just before Christmas 1936 the Red Cross turned up and decided to give her a paid-for health visitor. Part of her delight and relief is demonstrated by how she describes the arrival of the Red Cross health visitor, who turned up unexpectedly on Christmas day afternoon. Hilda had slipped away from her guests at Rasulia with the intention of visiting the English social worker Miss Caton, who worked for the India Village Welfare Society, who was at Jamai. Unexpectedly, she found herself enthusiastically greeted at the ashram since there were celebrations for Barra Din, the Indian version of Christmas, in full swing. The trees and bushes at Jamai were bright with decorations, and she was heavily garlanded. At this point she noticed a tonga in front of the ashram,

> and a stout, soncy-looking Indian, disconsolately pacing the paths—the new Red Cross Health Visitor ... She is a great success—she harangues the Bais with humour and rhetoric in a hearty Indian Village voice. (Don't talk about India's dumb millions, they don't really exist). They answer with cheerful comments. She has our third cottage [at the Ashram]. We are now going round to different villages introducing her—each expedition an event in itself. We gather the women together and she addresses them and then proceeds to give out medicines.[184]

When the dispensary was opened, there was an altogether different celebration, geared towards attracting publicity in the hope of potential donors. Hilda had managed to get Lady Bhose[185] to come to the opening ceremony. Lady Bhose was Scottish (Margaret Wilkins Stott), a pioneer woman doctor who had qualified at St Andrews University College, Dundee and had come out to India as a Baptist medical missionary around the time that Hilda was setting up the Bristol Settlement. Hilda described the proceedings as decidedly 'posh' and was later able to announce that she had had a donation from a wealthy Bombay donor for the purchase of medicines. In a very short space of time, Cashmore had got herself integrated amongst the British and Indian circles working in public health and education. A final example of her serendipitous methods of operating was her response to a young Sadhu, Jesu Das Tivari, who had been recommended to go to Rasulia by Verrier Elwin, a former missionary who became an anthropologist, ethnologist and tribal activist. She described the Sadhu thus:

> He is a Brahmin, of education and position, and of singular charm, who has become a Christian without ceasing to love and study the great Bhakti poets and his own inheritance. He is twenty-five and is reading Mysticism and Quakerism here, two subjects not so far apart. I have been coaching him regularly.[186]

This was the desired objective: reconciliation between the cultures of East and West. He was staying for a month, so she immediately also found him a job: to sort out the library and keep the files on it up to date.

In fact, these last months of 1936 were halcyon days for Hilda, with success after success, especially when Jamai became fully operational. She wrote to Marian:

> I have nearly had my head turned by compliments from all these people, who have come to the Summer Schools—they simply love Jamai—can't believe it! The Indian students said they had not thought it possible English people could live simply like that, Professor Patil, very experienced student of Indian Villages, went around ours the last day by himself, and came back … saying now he knew why I had chosen Jamai. He said the people were unique in these Villages, the conditions they lived in so wretched, and they themselves such fine men and women, the soil so good, the cultivation so utterly miserable, the beauty of it all so great.[187]

A scene she wrote about captures her mood. At the last summer school in November, CF Andrews himself turned up. He had been staying in Gandhi's village ashram, near Wardha. She met him at the station and "took him and the young Christian Sadhu out to Jamai, CFA all in white khaddar, brother Jesu Das in saffron. They looked as they walked through the jungle as if they had come straight out of the Bible, CFA a gentle old prophet with his long beard, and Jesu Das, tall and young and straight".[188]

Hilda was also fortunate that it was in December 1936 that Carl Heath, chair of the British Friends Service Committee, turned up with his wife. Without any effort on her part, they were both charmed and impressed by what she had achieved in Rasulia and Jamai. It is not clear, but they may have advised Hilda to go to London for the hot season in 1937 to give her report to the Committee in person and make a plea for the continued support of her ventures after she left India at the end of that year. She certainly decided to do that, and to take a furlough of 5 months instead of the usual 3 months summer break she had had in Ootacamund in 1935, when she also travelled around south India, and Naini Tal, the hill station for civil servants of UP, where she had gone in the summer of 1936. In London in 1937, she got the full backing of the Quakers and spent the rest of the time trying to find voluntary donors who would provide her settlement and ashram with some income. On her return to India in November 1937 with her latest assistant, Kathleen Noakes, she found herself facing new challenges. On the negative side, Rasulia had slipped back to a state of chaos and inertia amongst the staff in her absence and worse, had been hit by an outbreak of malaria, while Jamai villages were being threatened by a cholera outbreak. On the plus side, there was one last thing she wished to do—to connect the Jamai villages to the growing movements for village improvements, such as the United Provinces Government's Village Uplift Programme.

It was the negative side that hit first on her return. She was picked up at the station by her driver. The very next day he, and his small son, became sick with malaria. The cook then also went down with it. Hilda had to engage a temporary driver and cook straight away. She found getting Rasulia operational again difficult.

> I have been struggling with getting things going that have gone to rest—looking after pools of standing water with kerosene—getting servants to work after long idleness—dealing with rats which are eating everything as usual—even the sheets on my bed and my sponge bag and soap on my stand. It is all great fun, if a little strenuous at times.[189]

The latter comment is the only note of down-heartedness recorded in all the letters Marian Pease published. Five days later Hilda wrote: "I feel there are stages in a person's real life when what they are doing is ending … and that there is a time … to trust your past life to others and to go forward on a new way will bring not frustration but fruition".[190] This tone is so different, it is possible she had contracted malaria herself as she certainly had it when she returned to the UK. There is even a hint that she believed she caught it travelling in her car, saying that she was not using the "our old, half-dead, permanently malaria-stricken car".

It was no longer 'Prudence' but a wreck! But her resilience and strength of spirit was demonstrated yet again:

> Wonderful to relate, the young Mulgazar came over on Sunday, with the Mulgazar of Semri who wanted to buy this awful old motor car and so fell into my hands. He has now started a school under the District Council for 40 children including 3 girls. It began last month and is a very exciting event to me.[191]

The other bad event was the cholera outbreak which she set about combatting with her usual vigour. It had broken out in the brickworks but there were not many cases. She put potash she had been given by the new civil surgeon at Hosangabad twice in the well at Jamai and set off to Gatley, a large remote village, to do the same to the 30 odd wells there. She travelled there in an oxcart "to save ourselves, for these days in the Villages are very strenuous", another indication she was not entirely well. There was at least something to cheer her up. Mr Bhobe Ram, the brickworks director, invited her to his home to tell her he was going to "build some decent rooms for his Gond workers". It was another of her projects meeting with success. In just four weeks from her return, she had got everything at Rasulia functioning again and met the hazards of the malaria and cholera. She was able to write:

> It is astonishing to be enjoying this winter, without all the strain of these last years of working in the unknown. We are so happy, simple and apparently safe, a little community full of hope and good spirits.[192]

As the meetings and summer schools started up again, there was one last major project she wanted to engage with, the Village Uplift

Programme. She had already begun getting involved as early as March 1936, attending her first ten-day Uplift course at the experimental farm in Powarkhera, not far from Rasulia. She was the only woman and only English person there. By November 1936, she was considered 'an expert' by the District Commissioner, who found it hard to get support for this type of work. She organised an eight-day students' school over the Diwali holidays at Rasulia, bringing students from Indore College with Professor Patil, from Hislop College, with Professor Isaac and some students from the agricultural college at Nagpur. The course was based on discussions for a five-year plan for a group of villages and had invited "experts on co-operation, on money-lending Bills and Acts, on land tenure, agriculture, marketing, education and revenue, etc., etc., a very good programme and an hour's discussion".[193] In 1937, in her last months in India, she spent her time especially with Professor Patil, visiting villages in the oxcart. By now Professor Patil had also become a good friend and he helped her with the finishing touches to Jamai after the cholera outbreak: lining the well with stone, and the washing place, and the same for the cattle-drinking place in the middle of the village, all preventative measures against cholera in the future.

There was a last Friends Fellowship meeting and Dr Gravely from Madras and CF Andrews turned up again unexpectedly, presumably to say goodbye and to congratulate her on what she had achieved, though of course she did not put that down on paper. What she noted were the changes that had taken place since Andrews' first visit. No strolling through the jungle this time. "The Congress Leaders from Itarsi came and asked to be presented to CF Andrews. They looked picturesque in their Gandhi caps".[194] Hilda left Rasulia on the 5th December 1937, and made a slow journey, saying goodbye to friends *en route* to Nagpur where she had decided to attend the All India Women's Conference. This turned out to be a great contrast to her experience at the Karachi Conference she had attended on her arrival in India. She mentions two great changes. The first was very obvious. Now there were no more silk saris on display amongst the delegates. The Standing Committee had urged everyone to wear white saris, as a symbol of the absence of class distinctions in their organisation. The second was how references to the villages occurred all through the many discussions. "It was recognised that resolutions were not enough. Again and again, individual members were urged to get to work themselves in the villages...".[195]

Cashmore left India for good at the end of January 1938, arriving in England three weeks later. On her return she slipped quietly to Bristol where she found herself somewhere to live. Her health and strength had materially deteriorated. She was now suffering from severe arthritis and continuing bouts of malaria. When the Second World War broke out, although still very frail, Hilda was to be found yet again helping out at refugee and evacuee centres in Bristol, doing what she could in a civic and national emergency, right to the very last.[196]

In December 1940, H.C. was standing in the Library of the Friends Meeting House, Quakers' Friars receiving people bombed out from the neighbourhood, listening to their troubles, helping them to fill in forms and making plans for their immediate needs and at the same time directing the inexperienced efforts of a band of young helpers with the minimum of words and the maximum of effort.[197]

But by 1943, her illness became acute, she chose to go to London to avoid any publicity in Bristol, to stay with her sister Maud in Woolwich and to die there in her care.

Maud subsequently decided to follow Hilda's path to India, to offer her services as a nurse. In 1944, she became Sister Adeline in the Convent of Mount Tabor, Travancore, South India, continuing her midwifery and nursing work with mothers and babies. She had obviously been well advised by her sister of where to go. Hilda had ascertained in her visit to the south in 1935 that some of the maharajahs were proving better at modernising their states than the British. The Maharajah of Travancore was held up as a model leader of an efficient government and was thoroughly up to date. It is astonishing that Maud went to India after Hilda's death since she was only a year or two younger than Hilda, a measure perhaps of Hilda's influence and the deep religious faith they shared.

The Cashmore sisters were following a pattern that had been established by numbers of young, educated women who, in the early twentieth century, had gone out to India to use their skills as doctors, nurses and social workers.[198] Hilda and her sister Maud were different in that they both went out *after* undertaking their major lifework of service in their own country, Maud as a pioneer in creating the modern profession of midwifery. Hilda, however, was also decidedly untypical in what she achieved in the settlement movement: in Bristol, in Manchester, as President of the British Association of Residential Settlements and, spectacularly, what she achieved in India. It is only due to her determined Quaker modesty that her name has remained relatively unknown.

Epilogue

Reflections on the legacy of settlement work since the Second World War

Hilda Cashmore deeply hoped that her settlement work would have a legacy. She was not concerned about the actual buildings she established so much as establishing an understanding that, in cities and countryside, what mattered was the future of people's lives, not just in material gains but in their chances of personal development in rapidly changing times. Her experiences in England and India confirmed her in her belief that there needed to be constant reconciliation between people from different cultural contexts and traditions and change over time. Her pioneering work in Bristol was her touchstone. At the very moment when, in India, she was trying to set up her settlement and ashram, it was her experience of working in Bristol that came to her mind. She wrote: "My private idea is … that Rasulia might always be the 'Social Settlement' side of the work … and that the real site [the ashram] should be the centre for the intimate work for that group of villages—rather like Barton Hill is to Rotha Clay at Shirehampton"[199]. Settlement and outreach activities developed alongside the key changes taking place. In Barton Hill, at the time of Hilda Cashmore's death in the middle of the Second World War, her ideas and beliefs were to be tested as never before. Incredibly, the resilience of her primary ideas was to survive as the institutional forms around them changed.

At the centre of Cashmore's thinking was the concept of community that she had tried so hard to promote in the British Association of Residential Settlements. The Bristol Settlement retained its central residential community right through the war and most of the settlement activities. There is a tantalising glimpse of how the settlement operated during the war through the eyes of a New Zealander of Irish descent who got a post there from 1941–43. Winnie Davin had watched as the residents and people of Barton Hill became involved in the dark years of the bombing, looking to the future of the city. This account comes from a paper by Anna Davin who herself experienced life in the Bristol Settlement at the tender age of one to three (from 1941–43) in the company of her mother.[200] She uses her mother's accounts from letters in the family archive to explain why her mother chose to go there and how she found the experience. Winnie Davin had found herself alone in

Bristol University Settlement continued for
15 years after World War Two.

University students of the 1950s
collecting funds during Rag Week.

Britain with her toddler, and in need of employment, when her husband was drafted into the armed forces. She placed an advertisement in the *New Statesmen* for work and received four replies, three from women who wanted domestic help in their homes and one from the university settlement. She wrote to her husband that the last was advertised as

> unpaid work, living quarters provided free, at Bristol University Settlement, in a working-class district of Bristol. Activities include advising families in difficulties, Youth Shelter Clubs, educational work, arrangements for holidays, rest-breaks etc. They are shortly opening a convalescent home in the country for mothers and babies, so there is a lot of work in connection with this. They also do work listed as—Infant Welfare Centres, Play Centres, Childrens' Library, Clubs for Boys + Girls, After-Care Works, Crafts and Domestic Subjects, Drama, Housing Estate Work etc. There is a bungalow in the country for residents to go occasionally at weekends.

She thought this was a community settlement flexible enough to take in both her and her little daughter and offer them support in return for her labour.

She took the job, deciding not to be frightened by the heavy bombing of Bristol. She found she enjoyed living there and the training in social work she received from the warden. She could now add 'social worker' to her recognised skills. She gives vignettes of the individuals she met. The warden, still Hilda Jennings, was 'congenial, unconventional despite her position, and literary':

> She always curls up everywhere, as Mary [university friend from Dunedin] used to; and she's like her about clothes; + fearfully untidy about cigarette butts... She spends her time organising everything, serving on committees, + is Social Legislation lecturer to Social Science students at Bristol University.[201]

Another resident, Edith Cram, also a long-established resident, had picked up on the propaganda about the rebuilding of Bristol after the war and had organised an exhibition called 'Living in Cities'. Winnie Davin wrote:

...it was very successful, + has made many people interested to join discussion groups for reconstruction work. Bristol is so levelled to the ground that it is a marvellous theatre for planning, + the aim of making its citizens reconstruction-conscious seems to me laudable...There is already a liaison committee from whom the Corporation is demanding concrete proposals etc.—Women's knitting groups are to discuss what kind of housing they want, to visit housing estates, look at kitchen equipment etc—Infant Welfare mothers' meetings are to have talks about clinics, nurseries, best positions for playgrounds etc. W.E.A. groups discuss schools...

There was an optimistic hopefulness about all this, but it kept everyone thinking about a better future which was a powerful aid to getting through the present. The Settlement was also involved in the collection of data for William Beveridge's third report *Voluntary Action*,[202] that followed the famous 'Beveridge Report', *Social Insurance and Allied Services*, and his second report, *Full Employment in a Free Society*. He published the third report to show that he believed in the importance of voluntary work, in a society where state welfare had been adopted. But his idea of voluntary work was based on the self-help of individuals and communities of the kind institutionalised in the Victorian era. *Voluntary Action* was not financed by government, but by the National Deposit Friendly Society, the kind of voluntary society of which he heartily approved. 'Mutual aid' was the key element of one of the two sorts of voluntary impulses he selected as vital for a healthy society, the other being philanthropy. But of settlements, he roundly states: "Settlements have not accomplished—no-one can have imagined that they would accomplish directly—the objective of putting an end to social and economic segregation".[203]

Beveridge was pretty dismissive of the idealist tradition of social service of the pre-First World War days, as he had been even in his early days at Toynbee Hall.[204] As a good Liberal, he wanted the emphasis to be on individual self-reliance. He had no conception of how social groups might be integrated as cities grew or the importance of communication and reconciliation amongst civic society at large. If voluntary social services, such as settlements, did have a purpose at the time he was writing, it was to fill the gaps left by the welfare state until it was firmly established. They could also be useful for collecting social data when there were few professionals engaged in this. His summing up encapsulates his hugely optimistic vision of a future society, talking the talk of the old-style philanthropists, using the old terminology about settlements as 'the bridge between the two nations' which would be unnecessary now because of judicious physical planning:

> Ultimately, when all towns have been rebuilt as mixed communities, there may be no need for settlements, but until that happens, the need will continue. The settlements of today are not only essential centres for civic work but the means of conducting a continual survey of economic and social conditions through the eyes of those who live there.[205]

Jane Lewis has written extensively about the impact of the widely held belief that the 'welfare state' would solve all social problems and how this would affect voluntary social work and cause the residualisation of voluntary social work itself. She writes:

> Even though large numbers of social workers remained within the voluntary sector until the Seebohm reforms of the early 1970s, which created the personal social service departments in local authorities, they were increasingly paid professionals rather than volunteers.[206]

But she also points out that the crucial boundary was not between professional and voluntary work. It was instead 'between local provision, both voluntary and statutory, and welfare provided by central government'. This is where many of the women social workers had found themselves in the first half of the twentieth century. But nobody wanted to build on their experience. Lewis comments: "In this sense, women played little part in the construction of the welfare state"[207].

It was a grave loss. In the years up to the Second World War, the need to train social workers had been left to universities and some voluntary institutions, including the COS and they were all mostly dominated by women. The Department of Social Administration at the London School of Economics, both the earliest and by far the largest university department in the country, was the leading institution for training in social administration and for social workers. Most of the staff working there in the 1940s were women who had had their training in settlements. Many had engaged with key questions about recruiting and training social workers and how to develop social services. They had had almost half a century of experience in this work.[208] Chief among them currently was Eileen Younghusband, who had undertaken a survey of the need for training provisions for social workers in 1945, funded by the Carnegie Trust. In the five years that followed, she said the changes were so great that she brought out a second survey in 1951 on social work in Britain, also funded by Carnegie.[209]

Younghusband wanted to set up a new course at LSE and she looked to the USA, as Hilda Cashmore had done 30 odd years before, and to her American friend, Charlotte Towle, for help. Towle became special advisor for the LSE Carnegie course in training in social work. However, Towle's major book on the subject, *Common Human Needs,* was to run into trouble with the Federal Security Agency almost immediately after it was published in 1945.[210] The book unfortunately was branded as anti-American in the early 1950s during the US anti-communist witch-hunt. She had used the term 'socialised' for some activities and all copies of her book were withdrawn. There was no communist witch-hunt in the UK, but much lack of knowledge, a misunderstanding of women's contribution to social work and a belief that, anyway, in the new conditions of the post-war world, what was needed was for men to take the lead in sketching out the future of government social services. In 1950, Richard Titmuss, with no background in practical social service activity, was appointed to head the department at the LSE. Titmuss set his sights on influencing national social policy making, rather than exploring the locally based work of women in the past that had helped to identify key social problems and the conditions of those in need. There was a debate within his department, him against most of the women there.[211]

In his position of power, Titmuss won this debate and Younghusband did not get the promotion she deserved with her Carnegie project on *Social Work in Britain.*[212] Many of the women left to be replaced by a group of young men who earned the nickname of the 'Titmice', the three key figures being Titmuss himself, Brian Abel-Smith and Peter Townsend.[213] The Victorian gender divide, so hated by Cashmore, had returned in a different form in the mid-twentieth century. In Eileen Younghusband's second survey, she barely mentions settlements though they had been given many pages in her 1945 report. However, she does make one mention of settlements: in the appendix listing the provision of services, just one settlement, Bristol, gets an entry because of the quality of its Testamur qualification (Cashmore's invention). It was also the only place training youth workers. Bristol University Settlement was still training students within the context of the city, developing services alongside the people from 'the bottom up', in collaboration with the local city authorities. The implications of the changes in state legislation were to be dramatic on the ground, with the increasing control of the state and private financial interests over courses of action at the local level.[214] Of course, with the benefit of hindsight, it is also clear that there was no perception at that time of what could happen in the future if the government began to unpick the idea of state welfare, or began to use commercial suppliers to deliver state welfare, and there was nothing coherent working to meet local social needs not covered by this system.

The university settlements of Liverpool, Manchester and Birmingham, the three largest that had been established in England before Bristol, were caught up in these changes. Fortunately for them, they were able to establish their own momentum before the Second World War, sustained by the size, wealth and charitable traditions of their cities. Over a million in population in all three cases, they had adopted the kind of role that, in 1934, Elizabeth Macadam had outlined in *The New Philanthropy*, taking the same path as government but privatising it, providing some kind of extra layer to state provision.[215] In these three cities, voluntary social work was absorbed by a not-for-profit professional organisation that became a central body for channelling funding and organising the distribution of voluntary resources, and some state resources, across the city and region. They have been made into companies with charitable status still working with local government, though needing to seek alternative methods of funding as local government resources have been cut.[216] They have all broken their links with their universities. Now their main support comes from their own earning capacities (usually supported by government) and private resources. They have all grown into the largest 'charities' in their cities and regions. Each has taken a unique path dictated by local conditions, history and culture, but all are still hugely important to the people, providing a range of supportive services, including education, training of all kinds, housing, leisure and well-being, as well as community services and facilities.

Yet despite these achievements, the oldest and most revered historian of Liverpool's charitable efforts across the nineteenth and twentieth century, Margaret Simey, was desolate at this outcome. Her last book, *From Rhetoric to Reality: a study of the work of FG D'Aeth*, written when she was in her late nineties, after a lifetime of social and political service, makes this clear. It is basically a *cri de coeur* for what she believes has been lost: the end objective of social service, the hope for a better economic and social democracy, inclusive of all citizens.[217] She is well-positioned to comment on the post-Second World War period as, after her pre-First World War and inter-war period experiences at the Liverpool Victoria Settlement and in professional social work, she threw herself heart and soul into making state services, as well as voluntary social welfare, work in the city. She became a Labour councillor and took many positions of responsibility, including chairing the police committee at the time of the Toxteth riots in 1981, in the hope that a strong supporter of social inclusiveness might make a difference.

She asks two questions: "What has all the work achieved?" and "Why do I suffer now from an even more passionate sense of injustice?" Her dismay is about the loss of moral compass in modern society that denies the "principle of the right of the individual to share a common responsibility for the well-being of all".[218] Now politicians use rhetoric to gain votes. Reality is a different matter. She makes the point that in her youth, women were politically excluded, but:

we are all politically excluded now, only more so. Old and young, men and women, black and white, we are no more than ballot-box fodder. Even our elected representatives, on whom we rely to articulate our wishes and meet our needs, dumbly acquiesce in their subjection to a system geared to the values of the market-place. There is no scope for philanthropy. We are a disinherited society, deeply deprived of our right to active membership of the community to which we belong.[219]

She suggests that we are now back in the kind of situation that existed in her youth when problems seemed intractable. But then the young rebelled, filled with a "passion for social citizenship", and new initiatives were born. Hilda Cashmore's own work had been swept along by often youthful civic social commitment. The idea of creating and sustaining a vibrant social democracy had been behind the founding of the Bristol University Settlement and her whole career. Her vision of social democracy was one in which women took their place alongside

Young and old enjoy the facilities at Barton Hill.

men in terms of complete equality, regardless of race, colour or creed. Citizenship was for all.[220] She did not succeed on a national scale but her modest institution in Bristol, even as it has had to contract in its role in the city as a whole, has been able to keep closest of all the former university settlements to Cashmore's vision and objectives. Bristol, like the other provincial settlements, finally cut its ties with the university in 1970. At the final council meeting of the Bristol University Settlement, a new constitution and title were adopted for the now independent institution, the Bristol Settlement and Community Association, affiliated to the British Association of Settlements and Social Action. The university made a last goodwill gesture by building it a well-appointed new building for future community work in the Barton Hill neighbourhood, though there were to be no settlement residents. Here the Community Association has thrived, driven by the needs of new immigrants to Bristol from overseas as well as all the old problems of deprivation that have, as Simey noted, not gone away.

As for the concept of university settlements, there has recently been new interest in the twenty-first century. In 2001, two universities, Surrey and the London School of Economics, announced plans to set up graduate community work courses on the settlement model, though without residential facilities, in recognition of the importance in providing direct experience for training social workers and academics. Some local government bodies are also adopting the model as a possible way of making contact with people, for instance in Newcastle and Tower Hamlets in London.[221] In 2015, the educational settlement set up in the early 1920s by Cashmore's colleague, Lettice Jowitt, the Bensham Grove Settlement near Gateshead, received an injection of fresh funding, thus being given a new lease of life.[222] Also, after three years of renovation work, partly funded by the Heritage Lottery Fund, Toynbee Hall opened once again in 2018, as a residential settlement carrying on Barnett's ideal in the twenty-first century, providing free social services and giving place and space to those, this time both men and women, wishing to think creatively about future social policies.

Most happily of all, the University of Bristol is now in the process of creating a university settlement on its new campus near Temple Meads, designed to serve the complex communities in south and east Bristol. Pilot projects in the area, funded by a newly established Temple Quarter Enterprise Campus Public Engagement Fund, began in the summer of 2019. Research, education and collaboration may take place again in the spirit of Cashmore and Pease and the original university settlement of 1911. It does not amount to their early twentieth-century idealist vision of working towards a transformative future for the whole city, but it at least suggests that communication, contact and respect between helpers and helped is once again seen as a valid way forward. It is easy, as José Harris has suggested, to find the weaknesses of pioneers such as Hilda Cashmore with her optimism about the essential goodness of human nature. But Harris rightly suggests that:

> These objections do not alter the fact that idealism was the overarching philosophy of the early days of the welfare state; nor the fact that subsequent theorists of welfare have been conspicuously unsuccessful in constructing any more coherent, plausible and morally compelling alternative.[223]

Hilda Jennings quotes from Cashmore's contribution to the WEA handbook of 1918:

> The University Settlements of the future must be voluntary associations of men and women of all   classes, who have learnt that class consciousness is a weakness, not a strength; and class segregation impossible to men inspired with a common ideal. They will be the pioneers and the voluntary

element in a conscious attempt to work out a new democratic state—testing material prosperity by its power to develop full personality—a community in which human beings shall be ends in themselves; they will…create an atmosphere so alive, and yet so patient of difference, that a meeting ground is made for men and women of various classes and of conflicting views, a place for free discussion and the birth of new ideas.[224]

Afterword on archives for Hilda Cashmore and the Bristol Settlement

Hilda Cashmore's excessive modesty means that surviving primary sources on her life and achievements are thin. If anyone reading this pamphlet has copies of any papers or knows the whereabouts of any early records of the settlement, or of Cashmore, I do hope they will give copies to the Local History Collection in Bristol Central Library or the Bristol Archives[225] or hand them over to a member of the Barton Hill Local History Society who will ensure that they reach those destinations and can be preserved for the future.

Notes

1 Asa Briggs and A Macartney (1984) *Toynbee Hall. The First 100 years* (London: Routledge and Kegan Paul).

2 The number of military recruits who failed medical tests during the Boer War had triggered an Interdepartmental Committee on 'The Physical Deterioration of the Working Classes in Large Cities' in 1904.

3 Marian Pease (1945) *Hilda Cashmore 1876–1943*. Printed for private circulation by John Bellows Ltd, Gloucester.

4 June Hannam (2004) 'Alice Gregory 1867–1946', *Oxford Dictionary of National Biography*

5 A poignant example is the account written by Gladys Page-Wood. Pease, *op. cit.* 22–5.

6 Helen Meller (1976) *Leisure and the Changing City: Bristol 1870–1914* (London: Routledge and Kegan Paul) 130–4.

7 Edward R Pease (1916) *The History of the Fabian Society* (London: Routledge).

8 John B Thomas (2004) 'Marian Pease 1859–1954', *Oxford Dictionary of National Biography.* She studied courses in mathematics, heat, light, sound and political economy, and was limited in choice by a degree course which was geared towards the interests of male students.

9 *Memorials of Two Sisters, Susanna and Catherine Winkworth*, edited by Margaret J Shaen, (London: Longmans, Green, and Co.) 1908, 261.

10 William Whyte (2015) *Redbrick: a social and architectural history of Britain's civic universities* (Oxford: Oxford University Press).

11 Chamberlain, a large industrialist and mayor of Birmingham in the early 1870s, had moved into politics as a Liberal but, now in 1900, had changed sides and become a Unionist and key figure in the 'Khaki' Election of 1900, in the run up to the Boer War. His support for the new University of Birmingham was the last of his many philanthropic ventures in Birmingham.

12 A W Coats (1961) 'US Scholarship Comes of Age: the Louisiana Purchase Exhibition 1904' *Journal of the History of Ideas*, 22(3) 404–17.

13 Ashley was chairman of the Social Study Committee of the University of Birmingham. Later he became Professor of Economic History at the LSE, and one of the founders of the *Economic History Review.* Pat Hudson(ed) (2001) *Living Economic and Social History* EH-net Glasgow.

14 W J Ashley (1912) *The Yearbook of Social Progress for 1912: being a summary of recent legislation, official reports and voluntary effort, with regard to the welfare of the people* (London: Thomas Nelson and Sons). 526–7.

15 S A Barnett (February 1884) 'Settlements of University Men in Great Towns' *Nineteenth Century.*

16 M E Rose (1989) 'Settlements of University Men in Great Towns: university settlements in Manchester and Liverpool' *History Society of Lancashire and Cheshire Journal* 139, 137–160.

17 Eleanor Rathbone was to decide to devote her energies on a specific objective: family allowances. In Liverpool, during the First World War, she had seen the starving families of sailors, not yet back in port and no maintenance for their families. She wrote *The disinherited family: a plea for direct provision for the costs of child maintenance through family allowances.* Taking the political path, she became elected as an MP in 1929 in order to press her cause. Family allowances were passed into law in 1946, a few months

after her death.

18 Fiona L Bolam (2001) 'Working class life in Bradford 1900–1914: the philanthropic, political and personal responses to poverty with particular reference to women and children'. PhD thesis, University of Huddersfield. 29–118.

19 M Cahill and Tony Jowitt (1977) 'The New Philanthropy: The Emergence of the Bradford City Guild of Help' *Jnl Soc Pol.*, 9,3, 359–82.

20 Margaret Simey's last book was: *From Rhetoric to Reality: a study of the work of FG D'Aeth, social administrator* 2005 LU Press.

21 R Morris and H Russell (eds)(2010) *Rooted in the City: recollections and assessments of 100 years of voluntary action in Liverpool* LCVS.

22 The 1902 Act totally reformed state education: school boards were abolished including the higher-grade schools (important for girls); control passed to county council education authorities; and secondary education for boys only was introduced. The 1944 Education Act promised secondary education for girls, but it took some years to implement since schools had to be built.

23 Exact figures giving indication of the discrepancies in salaries between men and women can be found in Claire Davey (2012) 'Teacher Training in Bristol 1892–1930: a comparison across gender, and through time'. Best Undergraduate History Dissertation 2012.

24 D W Humphreys 'The education and training of teachers' in J G Macqueen and S W Taylor (eds) *University and Community: essays to mark the centenary of the founding of University College, Bristol* University of Bristol, 1976.

25 Women's Day Training College students + 60, women at the University College + 20 in actual numbers. *ibid* 43.

26 MM Falk, one of her students wrote: "she was to us a new kind of person. Everything seemed turned upside down as there unfolded before our astonished eyes a newer and larger world of mind and spirit than we could have imagined" (Falk, 8). Quoted from J B Thomas (2004) 'Marian Pease (1859–1954)' Oxford DNB.

27 Glasgow University Settlement was founded in 1889 and Edinburgh in 1905.

28 Hilda Jennings (1971) *University Settlement, Bristol: sixty years of change 1911–1971*, Bristol, University Settlement Bristol Community Association.

29 Harrow gives a detailed account of the formation of the Settlement and its relationship with the University *op. cit.* 387–411.

30 June Hannam (2019) *Mabel Tothill: Feminist, socialist, pacifist.* (Bristol: Bristol Radical Pamphleteer #45).

31 Tothill was the Hon.Sec of the East Bristol branch of the Civic League.

32 June Hannam, *op. cit.* 45.

33 H E Meller (1976) *Leisure and the Changing City, 1870–1914* London, Routledge and Kegan Paul, 204.

34 L Brierley and H Reid (2000) *Go home and do the washing! Three centuries of Pioneering Bristol Women* Bristol, Broadcast Books. I am indebted to June Hannam for this reference.

35 Mrs Miriam Badock founded the School in 1858, its ethos was proto-feminist and internationalist in outlook, particularly catering for boarders whose parents were posted overseas.

36 Elizabeth Wills' letters with Cashmore (1912) are now lost but discussed by Harrow *op. cit.* 404–405, endnotes 136,7,8,9.

37 Ernest Bevin was to become, after decades in the trade union movement, a major

player in the 1945 Labour government as Foreign Secretary dealing with the USSR and the US over war settlements.

38 She also had a small annuity from her father. She was representative of a number of women from wealthy backgrounds who chose to work for no pay. At the Settlement though, women, rich and poor, volunteered and were equally welcomed.

39 Content of the Testamur course is listed in the Biennial Report of the University Settlement Association 1917–19, *Local History Archive, Bristol Central Reference Library*. It is discussed in a later section.

40 Jowitt was not only a colleague, but she was also a great friend of Cashmore. She worked with her in France at the beginning of the First World War in the Quaker organization for relieving victims of war, and later went to the US to raise money for this work. She was an important member of the Federation of British Residential Settlements developed by Cashmore and started and sustained her own settlement as first warden of Bensham Grove, Gateshead from 1919, a residential educational settlement that is still thriving.

41 His nephew, Mr S H G Barnett, was a strong supporter of the Bristol University Settlement from the start and was for many years on the Settlement Council serving a long spell as treasurer.

42 The first Bishop of the newly revived See of Bristol, Dr George Forrest-Browne was later to be a supporter of the Bristol University Settlement. Pease (ed) *Hilda Cashmore*, 18.

43 *The Ideal City* was basically a rehash of a paper he wrote 'Town Councils and Social Reform', *Nineteenth Century*, Nov 1883, just 4 months before he published his first major paper on 'University Settlements' *ibid.* Feb 1884.

44 *The Ideal City* is reprinted in H E Meller (ed) (1979) *The Ideal City* (Leicester: Leicester University Press) 55–66.

45 Margaret Bondfield made this point in her warm tribute to Hilda Cashmore in Pease (ed) *op. cit.* 28.

46 Anticipation and excitement at what he had to say attracted 600 members to Manchester, an astonishing number since the Quakers were only 16,500 in total in the UK at that time. Rowntree's address is held to mark the beginning of a Quaker renaissance that lasted from 1895–1925 A E Southern, 'History and Quaker Renaissance: the vision of John Wilhelm Rowntree' n.d. available online, open access.

47 A E Southern (2010) 'The Rowntree History Series and the growth of liberal Quakerism 1895–1925', *etheses.bham.ac.uk*

48 Meller, *Leisure and the Changing City*, 132–34.

49 *Ibid.* 91–2.

50 *Ibid.* 206–37.

51 One of his students, William Straker, became a labour leader and trade unionist organiser regardless. He loved education but did not like paternalistic philanthropy and he set up a trade union in Frys, allied to the Dockers, registering labour independence. H P Smith 'Literature and Adult Education a century ago: panto pragmatics and Penny Readings', 48–32.

52 The Quakers' industry depended on importing supplies of cocoa beans and sugar from huge estates across the British Empire. Treatment of their black labour force was racist and certainly not on the same level as for their workers in the UK. Emma Robertson (2009), *Chocolate, Women and Empire: a social and cultural history* (Manchester: MUP). See also Catherine Hall (ed) (2000) *Cultures of Empire: colonizers in Britain and the Empire in the nineteenth and twentieth centuries* (Manchester: MUP).

53 Bentley B Gilbert (1973 edition) *The Evolution of National Insurance in Great Britain: the origins of the welfare state* (London: Michael Joseph Ltd).

54 Asa Briggs (1961) *Social Work and Social Action: a study of the work of Seebohm Rowntree 1871–1954* (London: Longmans).

55 Charles Booth (1889) *Life and Labour of the People in London,* 1st series: Poverty East, Central and South London. (London: Macmillan).

56 Beatrice Webb (1938 Penguin) *My Apprenticeship* Vol II 263–306. She states she became a socialist through working on this project.

57 B S Rowntree (1902 2nd ed) *Poverty: a study of town life* (London: Macmillan and Co). 1–4.

58 Robert C Reinders (1982) 'Toynbee Hall and the American Settlement Movement' *Social Service Review,* 56, 1, 39–54.

59 Pease *op. cit.* 16–17.

60 Jane Addams (1899) 'The Subtle problems of Charity' "Of the various struggles which a decade of residence in a settlement implies, none have made a more definite impression on my mind than the incredibly painful difficulties which involve both giver and recipient when one person asks charitable aid of another", *Atlantic Monthly,* February.

61 Information on her career, with a list of her publications, can be found in https://infed.org/mobi/mary-parker-follett-community-creative-experience-and-education/

62 A catechism in this instance, of the social work ethos of the Settlement, given in the form of question and answer.

63 Jenny Harrow found a copy of 'What is a Settlement?', published in the annual report 1910–11 of the Cooperative Social Settlement of New York, at the Bristol Settlement during her research. *op. cit.* 619 endnote 15.

64 José Harris (1989) 'The Webbs, the C.O.S. and Ratan Tata' M Bulmer, J Lewis, D Piachaud (eds) *The Goals of Social Policy* (London: Unwin Hymen) 51.

65 Quoted in 'Obituaries: Edward Johns Urwick 1867–1945', *Canadian Journal of Economic and Political Science/Revue Canadienne d'Economique et de Science Politique* 11,2 (May 1945) 265–268.

66 E J Urwick (1927) *The Social Good* (London: Methuen and Co Ltd). He tries to define this concept at book length.

67 Henrietta Barnett *op. cit.* 157.

68 *Ibid.* Chapter XXXV 469–83 We do not have any evidence from those who did not turn up!

69 Pease *op. cit.* 40.

70 Shelia Rowbotham *op. cit.* The women were very militant in 1889 but beaten by hostility from management and the inability of the Bristol factory to compete with Lancashire, 59–60.

71 For the history of the problems of this factory and the strikes which preceded it, see Mike Richardson (2016) *The Maltreated and the Malcontents: working in the Great Western Cotton Factory 1838–1914* (Bristol: Bristol Radical Pamphleteer #37).

72 Pease *op. cit.* 28–9. Bondfield at the time was leading the Women's Co-operative Guilds campaign for a minimum wage for women. She had been co-opted by Miss Llewellyn Davies as secretary of the Citizen sub-Committee of the Guild. M Bondfield (1948) *A Life's Work* (London: Hutchinson and Co) 128.

73 Laura Kelly (2015) *Irish women in Medicine c.1880s–1920s: origins, education and careers* (Manchester: Manchester University Press). Dr Baker had qualified in medicine

at Trinity College Dublin.

74 Geoffrey Finlayson (1990) 'A Moving Frontier: Voluntarism and the State in British Social Welfare 1911–1949 *Twentieth Century British History*, 1, 2, 183–206.

75 This was not a new idea in itself. The most well-known pioneer had been Margaret McMillan who had opened her first open-air school/health clinic for poor children in Bradford in 1911 and as a result, was the only woman to be asked to give a paper at the Ghent Urban Planning Congress in 1913, an event leading to the founding of the International Union of Cities. *Ghent Planning Congress 1913* intro. William Whyte, repr.IPH series, H. Meller (ed) (London: Routledge, 2014). *Communal Action in the nurture of children*, Section II 162–173.

76 A position he had achieved because of his work at the Congregational Broad Plains Mission as warden there in the 1890s when the mission was called 'the poor man's university'. There was no church built at the mission. Its work was entirely educational.

77 William Beveridge was present at an interview of Albert Mansbridge with Canon Barnett at Toynbee Hall. Barnett said when he left: "That man has fire in his belly". Support from Barnett and Toynbee Hall helped him to set up the Workers' Educational Association. William Beveridge (1948) *Voluntary Action* (London: George Allen and Unwin) 154.

78 Bradley *op. cit.* Boys' and girls' clubs had become a mainstay of settlement work in the first half of the twentieth century, 194.

79 Details on Bristol University Settlement's work are from Hilda Jennings, *Sixty Years, op. cit.*

80 *Ibid.* 15.

81 The Bristol Testamur was "the closest of anything associations achieved with the universities by the university settlements in this period", J R Harrow, *op. cit.* 410.

82 June Hannam (2004) 'Alice Sophia Gregory', *Oxford Dictionary of National Biography*. Cashmore worked through contact with her sister Maud, to make this happen.

83 Pease *op. cit.* 30.

84 Margaret Brasnett (1969) *Voluntary Social Action: a history of the National Council of Social Service 1919–1969*, Whitstable, published by the NCSS, 95.

85 Pease. *op. cit.*10.

86 A. Ruth Fry (1926) *A Quaker Adventure: the story of nine years' relief and reconstruction* (London: Nisbet and Co.Ltd).

87 Lettice Jowitt was to set up her own settlement at Bensham Grove near Gateshead and become a formidable and successful warden.

88 Marian Pease *op. cit.* 57.

89 *Ibid.* 12.

90 *Ibid.* 14–15.

91 Fry *op. cit.* Hilda got honourable mentions 12, 14–15.

92 Miss Walter gave her life to this work. In 1919 she fell ill with pneumonia and then caught influenza that proved fatal.

93 Deborah Dwork (1987) *War is Good for Babies and Other Young Children: a history of the infant and child welfare movement in England 1898–1918* (London and New York: Tavistock Publications) 213.

94 Gail Braybon (1981) *Women Workers in the First World War* (London: Croomhelm) 141.

95 Hilda Cashmore (1916) *The Possibilities of Industrial Welfare Work as a New Profession for Women. Being a paper read at Barnett House, Oxford* Special Collections

Womens' Archive, London School of Economics. Following paragraphs are in the present tense—a selection of the points she makes in her paper.

96 *Ibid.* 4.

97 *Ibid.* 1.

98 *Ibid.* 8–9.

99 *Ibid.* 10–12.

100 Hilda Jennings *op. cit* 28.

101 Clifton High School (6 lectures), Barry Training College, Gloucester Domestic Science School (3 lectures), Barnett House, Social Students' Union, London. Shirehampton and Bedminster Women's Co-operative Guild, WEA, Bristol branch, University of Bristol (12 lectures on local government) Canning Town Women's Settlement, Kingsley Hall, Bristol, Social Service Guild: Brotherhoods Meeting (2 lectures), Monmouth High School, Girls' Friendly Society, Shirehampton.

102 M.Pease (ed), *op. cit.* 25–27.

103 *Ibid.* 36–7.

104 Pease *op. cit.* 35–36.

105 *Ibid.* 69.

106 Letters from Alizon Fox, Frenchaymuseumarchives.co.uk, edited by Hubert C Fox, digitised by Gerald Franklin, Frenchay Tuckett Soc.

107 Helen Meller (2003) 'Housing and Town Planning, 1900–1939' C. Wrigley (ed) *A Companion to Early 20th Century Britain*, 388–405; W Ashworth (1954) *The Genesis of Modern British Town Planning: a study in economic and social history of the nineteenth and twentieth centuries* (London: Routledge and Kegan Paul Ltd).

108 Steve Hunt (2015 2nd edition) *Yesterday's Tomorrow: Bristol's Garden Suburbs* (Bristol: Bristol Radical Pamphleteer #8); Madge Dresseer (1984) 'Housing Policy in Bristol, 1919–30' M Daunton (ed) *Councillors and Tenants: local authority housing in English cities* (Leicester: Leicester University Press).

109 Hilda Jennings, *Sixty Years of change, op. cit.* 26.

110 *Ibid.* 26.

111 *The Settlement and its Pioneer Work in Bristol and Shirehampton*, pamphlet, n.d. (?1943) Bristol Record Office, 3–4.

112 http://infed.org/mobi/settlements.

113 charlesboothcentre.org.uk.

114 http://www.infed.org/henry-morris-village-colleges-and-community-schools.

115 Jeremy Burchardt (2012), 'State and Society in the English countryside: the rural community movement 1918–39, *Rural Society: economy, society and culture* 23, 1, 81–106.

116 Basnett *op. cit.* 19–36.

117 Madge Dresser (1984) 'Housing Policy in Bristol 1919–30' in M J Daunton, *Councillors and Tenants: Local Authority housing in English cities 1919–1930* (Leicester: Leicester University Press).

118 Not only more efficiently but also forcing families to adopt new ways of living and patterns of sociability. Gender ideologies were to come into focus. The most famous example was the 'Frankfurt kitchen' first to be designed by woman architect, Margarete Scheutte Linotzky 1926–27 though there were others especially in Munich. Leif Jarram (2006) 'Women, modernity and space in Weimar Germany' *Cultural Geographies* 13, 4, 538–56.

119 The Bishop of Kensington was the chairman of the Kensington Housing Association that employed Elizabeth Denby—the first women to break through the barrier from

voluntary worker to professional. Her book, *Europe Rehoused* (1938), became a best seller. See reprint (2015), introduction by Elizabeth Darling, *International Planning History Series*, H Meller (ed) (London: Routledge).

120 Dresser *op. cit.*

121 Pease *op. cit.* 30–1. Deedes was to play a great part working with Cashmore on the Federation of Residential Settlements and its successor, the British Association of Residential Settlements in the 1920s. He was also deeply involved in the formation of the National Council for Voluntary Social Service.

122 Itarsi was formed at the cross point of railways between Bombay to Calcutta and Delhi to Madras. It was located in Central Provinces in what is now Madhya Pradesh, and Cashmore was to become interested in the forest people, the Gonds.

123 Hilda Cashmore, Reprint of address on 'Settlements and Citizenship', read at the Annual Conference of the Federation of Residential Settlements, 29 June 1926. London Metropolitan Archives, City of London A/TOY/022/022/004.

124 *Ibid.* 2. All the following long quotations come from the same paper.

125 *Ibid.* 3.

126 see reference for list of Follett's publications in footnote 61.

127 The unease that operating this system caused, even those who sat on COS panels in charge of giving out relief, was made clear by Beatrice Webb. Beatrice Webb (1938 Pelican edition) *My Apprenticeship* Vol 1, 224.

128 C R Attlee (1920) *The Social Worker* (London: G Bell and Sons) 2–3.

129 She took this idea from Miss Follet's book *The New State*. Cashmore addressed the audience: "I assume then that you are familiar with the idea of the distinctive personality of this group made up not by the suppression of minority thinking, nor the domination of one leading mind, but by the integration of a number of individuals of varying temperaments, parties and interests into one whole. The life of the group is something larger than the individual life and has its own vitality and its own unique work. It is one integral whole and has a contribution to make to the life of the nation if it can get through." 'Settlements and Citizenship' *op. cit.* 4.

130 For example, Octavia Hill, the famous nineteenth century housing reformer, who inspired many who came after her with her work to improve the environmental context of the properties she managed. She used plants and greenery even in the heart of London's East End; created small local parks where she could; and saved areas of 'Outstanding Natural Beauty' through the National Trust, which she founded, and which has spread to every region of the UK.

131 The pioneer sociologist Patrick Geddes wrote in 1886: "but the social machine, which nobody knows how old, nobody knows how complex in its vast and innumerable ramifications—does anyone think of repairing it—yes: that's politics: but in detail, city by city, no; that would only be practical economics; and people are not interested in that." Helen Meller (1990) *Patrick Geddes* (London: Routledge) 24.

132 "The University Settlement had many roots in the life of the city. It has a Citizens Advice Bureau. It works in close cooperation with the churches and other religious bodies... There are close contacts with the Local Authority in education and other fields of social service etc" Quoted from pamphlet (1948): *The Settlement and its Pioneer Work in Bristol and Shirehampton*, 5.

133 A more contemporary example of her vision in practice occurred in the Ruhr in Germany when much of heavy industry, coal mines and steel works were collapsing at the end of the twentieth century. It was the students of the six Ruhr based universities,

working with the inhabitants of the de-industrialized areas, who led a concerted movement, with local, state and federal government help and support, to save the homes of the people and their communities and to recover the natural environment within a formerly heavily industrial region. The park and cultural use of buildings at Duisberg-Nord steelworks and the reuse of the Zollverein coal mine building for cultural purposes are examples of these successful outcomes. The Ruhr is now a tourist destination.

134 Bristol University Settlement offered another example of sensitivity to the needs of citizens during the war. Building on its Country Holidays for City Dwellers, started far back in 1923 with a hut and a field for family camping holidays, in the Second World War it set up a Rest Home for Mothers and Babies in 1942 at Caer Llan with funds channelled by the English-Speaking Union from the United States and the Bristol Lord Mayor's Fund. It was later moved to Wotton-under-Edge, to a house largely acquired by the efforts of university students. Pamphlet *Settlement and its Pioneer Work*. 4.

135 Jane Lewis (1996) 'The boundary between voluntary and statutory social service in the late 19th and early 20th centuries', *The Historical Journal* 39,1,155–77. Lewis suggests that in the interwar years, the partnership between the voluntary and statutory sectors was re-written to the detriment of the former and its broader vision for the future.

136 In 1926, a Quaker group went to Brynmawr in South Wales to do something to alleviate long-term suffering of the people trapped in desperate poverty with no jobs, bad housing and no future prospects. The Quakers set up small enterprises that gave jobs to a few. But the task was too big. Government legislation, the Special Areas Act (1932), was inadequate, failing to relieve the problem before the Second World War.

137 Margaret Brasnett (1969) *Voluntary Social Action* is the standard account on difficulties faced by the Council in the early years.

138 Helen Meller 'Housing and Town-Planning 1900–1939, in C. Wrigley (ed) (2009) *A Companion to Early Twentieth Century Britain.*

139 J J Mallon of Toynbee Hall was the central figure of the London Group. He had it minuted, when he returned from a leave of absence in 1927, that he was impressed "at the useful work that had been done in his absence", the period since Cashmore had taken over! The archive of the British Association of Settlements and Social Action Centres, Cadbury Research Library Special Collection, University of Birmingham Library, BAS/1/2, gives a detailed picture of Cashmore's personal struggle to move the Association forward. Following comments are all based on this material.

140 She was at the forefront of promoting the idea of citizenship rather than feminism that has been identified so clearly by Caitriona Beaumont (2000), 'Citizens not Feminists: the boundary negotiated between citizenship and feminism by mainstream women's organisations in England', *Women's History Review*, 9, 2, 411–426.

141 The following paragraphs are based on the BARS archive referenced above.

142 Andrew Chandler (2004) 'Deedes, Sir Wyndham Henry (1883–1956)' *Oxford Dictionary of National Biography.*

143 Captain Ellis was the treasurer who worked to solve the problems of funding new community centres.

144 What she had set up in Bristol continued under her successors. The university settlement in Shirehampton continued; in 1945 Miss Rotha Clay, the resident warden at University Settlement, Shirehampton from 1924–1944, helped towards the purchase of a fine Georgian building and garden to be a social centre for men and women

offering a wide range of educational and other activities. On another estate, Corner Cottage Settlement, Filwood Park, was set up, sponsored by the Council of Christian Churches and University Settlement. 'The Settlement and its pioneer work in Bristol and Shirehampton' pamphlet, Local History Library. In Manchester, she had success with the Wilbraham Association and the Newton Heath project, two smaller estates, the latter closest to the Settlement.

145 A B Robertson (2006) 'Tylecote [née Phythian] Dame Mabel' *Dictionary of National Biography*, Oxford University Press.

146 In 1947, Pilgrim Trust funding was withdrawn and by the 1950s the Settlement took the path towards becoming a Community Association and is still flourishing in the twenty-first century. The Spennymoor Settlement Archives, University of Durham Library, Archives and Special Collections GB–0033–SPE.

147 Mary D Stocks (1945) *Fifty Years in Every Street,* Chap VIII 'The Reign of Hilda Cashmore', 70–93.

148 John Stocks (1882–1937), ironically, was the kind of person Barnett would have wanted to recruit for Toynbee Hall. An ex-Rugby schoolboy, he was from the same school and same generation as R H Tawney (1880–1962) who did so much to promote adult education at Toynbee Hall. Stocks had run the Rugby Boys' Club and was an active member of the Workers' Educational Association.

149 Mary Stocks was only person to offer some criticisms of Cashmore in the Memorial Volume, "she was not at her best in committees", Pease, *op. cit*, 33. Stocks also felt her husband's contribution had been underacknowledged!

150 M D Stocks (1945) *Fifty Years in Every Street: the story of Manchester University Settlement.* (Manchester: Manchester University Press) 66.

151 He wrote the influential propaganda book: T C Horsfall (1904), *The Improvements of the Dwellings and the Surroundings of the People: the Example of Germany* (Manchester: Manchester University Press).

152 Winifred Gill Archive, Oxford Bodlian Libraries MS/6241/1 deposited in 2009.

153 Fry had inherited a large bequest from J S Fry of Bristol, his uncle, who died in 1913. The Omega Gallery lasted from 1913–1919 and gained the reputation of being the centre of a special kind of British modernism in art and design.

154 Margery Fry had been able to leave her job running a hall of residence in Birmingham because she, like her brother, had had a substantial legacy from J S Fry of Bristol.

155 T. Kelly (1992 3rd ed) *A History of Adult Education in Great Britain* (Liverpool: Liverpool University Press) 277.

156 Cashmore helped to get Spennymoor Settlement, devoted to arts and drama, started in 1931 and had a role in appointing the Farrells, husband and wife, in her capacity as chair of BARS, getting funding from the Pilgrim Trust.

157 Pease *op. cit.* 38.

158 Phil Childs (2020) 'Blacktown, Mass Observation and the dynamics of Voluntary Action in mid twentieth century England' *The Historical Journal*, 63, 3, 754–76. Papers of the Nuffield College, *Social Reconstruction Survey*, Library of Nuffield College, Oxford. Initially led by G D H Cole 1941–1955 Mss NCRS. Available online.

159 Ann Hughes and Karen Hunt, 'A culture transformed? Women's lives in Wythenshawe in the 1930s' in A Davies and S Fielding (eds) (1992) *Worker's World. Cultures and Communities in Manchester and Salford 1880–1939* (Manchester: Manchester University Press) 74–101.

160 Brasnett *op. cit.* 19–36.

161 Georgina Brewis (2014) *A social history of student volunteering: Britain and beyond 1880–1980* (New York: Palgrave Macmillan) 13–89.

162 Brewis, *op. cit.* Brewis suggests that: "in India and China … student social service was often frustrated by the gulfs of experience and understanding between students and the impoverished groups of people they tried to help", 44.

163 Basnett *op. cit.* 41–46.

164 Pease, *op. cit.* 75.

165 Pease, *op. cit.* 75.

166 Pease, *op. cit.* 30–1.

167 George Woodcock (1972) *Gandhi* (London: William Collins and Sons) 65.

168 Pease, *op. cit.* 75–76.

169 *Ibid.* 77.

170 Pease, *op. cit.* 79.

171 *Ibid.* 81.

172 *Ibid.* 84.

173 *Ibid.* 85.

174 Pease, *op. cit.* 81.

175 Pease, *op. cit.* 89.

176 Pease, *op. cit.* 90.

177 *Ibid.* 92.

178 *Ibid.* 98.

179 A tonga is a two-wheeled, light, horse-drawn cart with a canopy, in fact, like a horse drawn rickshaw, a cheap means of travel.

180 Pease, *op. cit.* 98.

181 Pease, *op. cit.* 100.

182 Andrews went to South Africa before the First World War, at Gandhi's father's request to bring his son back to India. He forged a life-long friendship with Gandhi and shared with him his other life-long passion for promoting education for all in preparation for the future, living in an independent India. He was the leading English figure connecting the British and Indians in social work and education outside of politics. His book of 1912 *The Renaissance of India* (London: Church Missionary Society) was widely used as a text, posing the challenge of the future: educating Indians for taking over the country when the British left. His close connection with Gandhi was important to both men.

183 Pease, *op. cit.* 107.

184 Pease, *op. cit.* 114.

185 Lady Bhose's husband was an ICS officer who had risen in the ranks and awarded a KCIE—a Knight Commander of the Indian Empire, Queen Victoria's strange parallel system of honours for service in India.

186 Pease, *op. cit.* 109.

187 *Ibid.* 111.

188 *Ibid.* 112.

189 Pease, *op. cit.* 117.

190 *Ibid.* 118.

191 *Ibid.* 119.

192 Pease, *op. cit.* 120.

193 *Ibid.* 110.

194 *Ibid*. 120.

195 Pease, *op. cit.* 121.

196 John B Thomas, 'Hilda Cashmore', *Dictionary of National Biography*, lists that in 1940, she worked for Bristol Council of Refugees, working with both the Non-Aryan Relief Committee of Bristol Council of Churches and the Jewish Relief Committee. She also worked with Bristol Committee of the Friends Relief Service, and from 1941 to her death as district service organizer of the Women's Voluntary Service in east Bristol.

197 Penelope Jenkin writing in Pease, *op. cit* 50–56.

198 Georgina Brewis (2014) *A social history of student volunteering: Britain and beyond, 1880-1980* (New York: Palgrave Macmillan).

199 Pease, *op. cit.* 91.

200 Anna Davin 'Community, Life-cycle, Diaspora: A Daughter's View' in B Brookes and D Page (eds) (2002) *Communities of Women: Historical Perspectives* (Dunedin: University of Otago Press) 21–24. Anna Davin grew up to have a distinguished career as a radical historian. She played a particularly important role in establishing Labour History. She was in the initial editorial collective of the *History Workshop Journal* and was a pioneer of Womens' History, helping to organize the first conference of Womens' History and supporting the Womens' History Network at its very beginning. Her many publications and research mostly concentrated on putting the lives of ordinary and poor people to the fore, eg: *Growing Up Poor: Home, School and Street in London 1870– 1914* (1996). She has been an inspiration to countless scholars and also to many women interested in history with no academic training who just loved women's history.

201 In her turn, Hilda Jennings writes warmly about Mrs Davin: "a New Zealander, whose husband was serving abroad. With her little girl, aged 18 months, Mrs Davin brought gaiety and the spirit of enterprise to all she undertook. Indeed, she said that she chose the Settlement "because it offered Air raids and an opportunity to pioneer in meeting new wartime needs". *Bristol University Settlement: Sixty Years of Change*, 33–4.

202 The Settlement had also been involved in collecting data for another ambitious survey: the Nuffield College, Oxford, Social Reconstruction Survey. Its prime instigator and designer of the survey, G D H Cole, then sub-warden of Nuffield College, was wildly ambitious hoping to cover all demographic, economic and social data as a guide for post-Second World War policy making. The extent of the survey is evident from the papers of the Nuffield College Social Reconstruction Survey, Library of Nuffield College, Oxford. The Treasury supported it during its first years, 1941-2, but the funding stopped as expenses grew and objectives became less and less clear. Reference to Bristol University Settlement undertaking collection of evidence for Nuffield Survey: pamphlet, *The Settlement and its Pioneer Work in Bristol and Shirehampton* n.d., 5.

203 Lord Beveridge (1948) *Voluntary Action: a report on methods of social advance* London, George Allen and Unwin, 131

204 Lord Beveridge (1947) *India Called Them* (London: George Allen & Unwin). In this biography of his parents, Beveridge lauds his mother and her work educating Indian girls (which she did drawing a clear racial line between herself and her charges) whilst his father was in the Bengal Civil Service. Beveridge and his sisters were all born in India. This was a very different context to that of Cashmore and her hopes of education for women.

205 *Ibid*. 132.

206 Jane Lewis (1996) 'Women, social work and social welfare in twentieth century

Britain: from (unpaid) influence to (paid) oblivion' in M Daunton (ed) *Charity, Self-Interest and Welfare in the English Past* (New York: St Martin's Press).

207 Jane Lewis (1994) 'Gender, the Family and Women's Agency in the Building of States: the British case' *Social History* 19,1,37–55.

208 E J Urwick had been appointed in 1910 as the first Director of the Department of Social Sciences and Social Administration. In 1912 Clement Attlee briefly worked as a tutor in the Department.

209 Eileen L Younghusband (1951) *Social Work in Britain: a supplementary report on the Employment and Training of Social Workers* published by Carnegie Trust. She discusses the role of universities and settlements (as representatives of voluntary work) in training. The nub of the problem is that universities are not in the business of training professional workers with specific practical skills. This breakdown in the relationship (that Cashmore had so successfully implanted in Bristol) was due to two factors: the emergence of social work as a series of specialized professions and the swing from voluntary to state employment. Paragraphs 496–500 (p. 178–9) also relevant 460–466 (p. 162–5).

210 In what was to become the Department of Health and Human Services.

211 Oakley *op. cit*, 173–93.

212 Ann Oakley (2014) *Father and Daughter: patriarchy, gender and social science* (Bristol: Policy Press) 123–48.

213 Brian Abel-Smith's biographer, Sally Sheard, says the welfare state we have in Britain today is essentially the dream of three men: Richard Titmuss, Peter Townsend and Brian Abel-Smith', *ibid*. 85.

214 Recent research on voluntary provision for medical services before the Welfare State show that in the large cities provision was often very good. The focus on the city stimulated local philanthropy. Nick Hayes and Barry Doyle (2013) 'Eggs, rags and whist drives: popular munificence and the development of provincial medical voluntarism between the wars' *Historical Research* 86. 234, 712–40. B M Doyle (2014) *The politics of Hospital Provision in early 20th century Britain* (Abingdon: Taylor and Francis).

215 See above, 10.

216 A recent study of the NCVO has called into question the model for that organization as currently being unfit for purpose in twenty-first century circumstances. Justin Davis Smith (2019) *100 years of the NCVO and Voluntary Action: Idealists and Realists* (Palgrave Macmillan) 265–279.

217 Margaret Simey, edited by David Bingham (2005) *From Rhetoric to Reality: a study of the work of F G D'Aeth, Social Administrator* (Liverpool: Liverpool University Press).

218 *Ibid*. 1–2.

219 Simey, *op. cit*. 3.

220 Hilda Jennings (1971) *University Settlement, Bristol: sixty years of change 1911–1971* (Bristol: University Settlement Bristol Community Association).

221 *The Guardian*, 'University of Life', article on the return of the Victorian idea of the Settlement, theguardian.com, 11 Apr 2001.

222 For details see www.benshamgrove.org.uk.There is a photo of Jowitt with her co-workers in 1920 entitled 'A bunch of scary women'!

223 José Harris (1992) 'Political Thought and the Welfare State 1870–1940: an intellectual framework for British Social Policy' *Past and Present*, Vol 135, 14.

224 Jennings *op. cit*. 5–6.

225 All easy to contact online: Bristol Local History and the Bristol Archives: Bristol.

library.service@bristol.gov.uk; www.bristolmuseums.org.uk/bristolarchives; there is also the Bristol University Archives, see the University website; and Barton Hill Local History: www.bhhg.co.uk.

Bibliography

Primary sources

Hilda Cashmore (1916) *The Possibilities of Industrial Welfare Work as a New Profession for Women. Being a paper read at Barnett House, Oxford*, Special Collections, Women's Archive, London School of Economics

Cashmore H (1926) 'Settlements and Citizenship' A/TOY/022/022/044 London Metropolitan Archives Letters from Alizon Fox, Frenchaymuseumarchives. co.uk, edited by Hubert C Fox, digitised by Gerald Franklin, Frenchay Tuckett Soc.

The archive of the British Association of Settlements and Social Action Centres, Cadbury Research Library Special Collection, University of Birmingham Library, BAS/1/2

Minutes of Meetings of University Settlement Association 1917–19, Local History Library, Bristol Central Library

Author (probably) Hilda Jennings 1948 'The Settlement and its Pioneer Work in Bristol and Shirehampton', University Settlement Bristol

Bristol Local History Library, Central Library, College Green, Bristol (numerous contemporary sources)

Bristol Record Office, Pamphlet 1637(a)

Papers of the Nuffield College Social Reconstruction Survey, Library of Nuffield College, Oxford Initially led by G D H Cole, 1941–1955 MSS.NCRS Available online

Contemporary texts

Attlee, C R (1920) *(The) Social Worker* London, G Bell and Sons, Ltd.

Attlee, C R (1954) *As it happened: the memoirs of the Rt.Hon. C.R.Attlee* London, William Heinemann

Ashley, W J (ed) (1912) *The Year-Book of Social Progress for 1912: being a summary of recent legislation, official reports, and voluntary effort, with regard to the welfare of the people* London, Edinburgh, Dublin, Manchester, Leeds and New York, Thomas Nelson and Sons

Barnett, S A and H (1888) *Practicable Socialism: essays in social reform* London and New York, Longmans, Green & Co

Barnett, S A and H (1909) *Towards Social Reform* London, T Fisher Unwin

Barnett, Henrietta (1921 edition) *Canon Barnett: his life, work and friends, By his wife* London, John Murray

Beveridge, Sir William (1942) *Social Insurance and Allied Services a Report: presented to Parliament by Command of His Majesty Nov 1942* HMSO

Beveridge, Lord (1948) *Voluntary Action: a report on methods of social advance* London, George Allen & Unwin Ltd.

Beveridge, Lord and Wells A F (1949) *The Evidence for Voluntary Action: being memoranda by organisations and individuals and other material relevant to Voluntary Action* London, George Allen and Unwin Ltd.

Beveridge, Lord (1947) *India Called Them* London, George Allen & Unwin Ltd.

Black, C (1915) *Married Women's Work* reprinted by Virago Press 1983

Fry, A Ruth (1926) *A Quaker Adventure: the story of nine years' relief and reconstruction* London, Nisbet and Co Ltd.

Hill, Octavia (2nd Edition 1883) *Homes of the London Poor,* and Mearns, Andrew (1883) *The Bitter Cry of Outcast London: an inquiry into the condition of the abject poor,* Note by W H Chaloner (1970) Frank Cass and Co

Jennings Hilda (1962) *Societies in the Making: a study of development and redevelopment within a county borough* London, Routledge and Kegan Paul

Jennings Hilda (1971) *Sixty Years of Change: the Bristol University Settlement 1911–1971* Bristol, University Settlement Bristol Community Association

Macadam, Elizabeth (1934) *The New Philanthropy: a study of the relations between the statutory and voluntary social services* London, George Allen and Unwin Ltd.

Pease, Marion (1945) *Hilda Cashmore 1876–1943* Printed for private circulation by John Bellows Ltd., Gloucester

Rowntree, B Seebohm (1902) *Poverty: A Study of Town Life* London, Macmillan and Co

Spring Rice, Margery (1939) *Working-class Wives, Their Health and Conditions,* London, Pelican Press

Stocks, M D (1956 2nd edition) *Fifty Years in Every Street: the story of the Manchester University Settlement* Manchester, Manchester University Press

Stocks M D (1921) *The Meaning of Family Endowment* London, Labour Publishing Co. Ltd.

Urwick E J (1927) *The Social Good* London, Methuen and Co. Ltd.

Wilson, James M (1932) *An Autobiography 1836–1931* London, Sidgwick and Jackson Ltd.

Younghusband, Eileen L (1951) *Social Work in Britain: a supplementary report on the employment and training of social workers* Carnegie United Kingdom Trust, Dunfermline, printed in Edinburgh, T and A Constable Ltd.

Secondary literature

W H G Armytage (1955) *Civic Universities: aspects of a British Tradition* London, Ernest Benn Ltd.

Billis, David and Harris, Margaret (eds) (1996) *Voluntary Agencies: Challenges of Organisation and Management* Basingstoke, Macmillan

Bradley, Katherine (2016 edition) *Poverty, philanthropy and the state: charities and the working classes in London 1918–79* Manchester, Manchester University Press

Brewis, Georgina Brewis, (2014) *A Social History of Student Volunteering: Britain and Beyond 1880–1980* New York, Palgrave Macmillan

Brasnett, Margaret (1969) A history of the National Council of Social Service 1919–1969 London, NCSS

Briggs, A (1963) *Victorian Cities* London, Odhams Books Ltd.

Briggs, A and Macartney, A (1984) *Toynbee Hall, The first hundred years* London, Routledge and Kegan Paul

Bulmer, Martin, Lewis, Jane, Piachaud, David (1989) *The Goals of Social Policy* London, Unwin Hymen Ltd.

Den Otter, Sandra (1996) *British Idealism and Social Explanation: a study in Late Victorian Thought* Oxford, Clarendon Press

Dresser, M and Ollerenshaw, P (eds) (1996) *The Making of Modern Bristol* Tiverton, Redcliffe Press

Dresser, Madge (2016) *Women and the City: Bristol 1373–2000* Regional History Centre UWE, Redcliffe Press Ltd.

Dyhouse, Carol (1989) *Feminism and the Family in England 1880–1939* Oxford, Basil Blackwell

Dyhouse, Carol (1995) *No distinction of sex? Women in British Universities 1870–1939* London UCL Press

Dyhouse, Carol (2006) *Students: a gendered history* Abingdon, Routledge

Gorsky, Martin (1999) *Patterns of Philanthropy: Charity and Society in Nineteenth Century Bristol* RHS, The Boydell Press

Harris, José (1997 2nd edition) *William Beveridge: A biography* Oxford, Clarendon

Holloway, G (2005) *Women and Work in Britain since 1840* Routledge, Abingdon

Householder van Horn, S (1988) *Women, Work and Fertility 1900–1986* New York University Press, New York and London

Jones, Helen (c1994) *Duty and Citizenship: the correspondence and political papers of Violet Markham 1896–1953* London, Historians' Press

Kelly, Thomas (1992 3rd edition) *A History of Adult Education in Great Britain from the middle ages to the twentieth century* Liverpool, Liverpool University Press

Lewis, Jane (1984) *Women in England 1870–1950: sexual division and social change* Brighton, Wheatsheaf Books

Lewis, Jane (1991) *Women and Social Action in Victorian and Edwardian England* Aldershot, Edward Elgar

Macqueen, J G, Taylor, SW (eds) (1976) *University and Community: Essays to mark the Centenary of the founding of University College, Bristol* Bristol, University of Bristol

Malpass, Peter (2019) *The Making of Victorian Bristol* Woodbridge, The Boydell Press

Marshall, Mary Paley (1947) *What I Remember* Cambridge, Cambridge University Press

Meacham, Standish (1987) *Toynbee Hall and Social Reform, 1880–1914: The Search for Community* New Haven, Conn: Yale University Press

Meller, H E (1976 repr 2013) *Leisure and the Changing City, 1870–1914* London, Routledge and Kegan Paul

Morris R and Russell H (eds) (2010) *Rooted in the City: recollections and assessments of voluntary action in Liverpool* Liverpool, Liverpool Charity and Voluntary Services

Oakley, Ann (2014) *Father and Daughter: Patriarchy, Gender and Social Science* Bristol, Policy Press

Otter, Sandra M Den (1996) *British Idealism and Social Explanation: a study in Late Victorian Thought* Oxford, Clarendon Press

Page, Robert M and Silburn Richard (eds) (1998) *British Social Welfare in the Twentieth Century* Basingstoke, Macmillan

Pedersen, Susan and Mandler, Peter (eds) (1994) *After the Victorians: private conscience and public duty in modern Britain* London and New York, Routledge

Pimlott, J A R (1935) *Toynbee Hall. Fifty years of social progress 1884 – 1934* London, Dent

Richter Melvin (1964) *The Politics of Conscience: T H Green and His Age* London, Weidenfeld and Nicolson

Rowbotham, Sheila (2016) *Rebel Crossings: New Women, Free Lovers, and Radicals in Britain and the United States* London, Verso

Simey, Margaret (1951) *Charitable Effort in Liverpool in the Nineteenth Century* reprinted 1992, Liverpool, LUP

Simey, Margaret (1996) *The Disinherited Society: a personal view of social responsibility in Liverpool during the Twentieth Century* Liverpool, Liverpool University Press

Simey, Margaret (ed. David Bingham) (2005) *From Rhetoric to Reality: a study of the work of F G D'Aeth, Social Administrator* Liverpool, Liverpool University Press

Vicinus, Martha (1985) *Independent Women: work and community for single women 1850–1920* London, Virago

Webb, Beatrice (1938 Pelican edition) *My Apprenticeship* Vol 1 and 2

Whyte, William (2015) *Redbrick: a social and architectural history of Britain's civic universities* Oxford, Oxford University Press

Widdowson, Frances (2nd edition 1983) *Going up into the next class: women and elementary teacher training 1840–1914* London Hutchinson with the Women's Research and Resources Centre

Articles and chapters

Abrams, Laura S and Curran, Laura (2004) 'Between Women: Gender and Social Work in historical perspective' *Social Service Review,* 78, Sept, 429–446

Barnett S A (1883) 'University Settlements in our Great Towns' *Nineteenth Century,* 26, 278

Barnett, S A (1895) 'University Settlements' *Nineteenth Century* Dec 1015–24

Barnett, S A (1897) 'The Ways of "Settlements" and of "Missions" *The Nineteenth Century: a monthly review* Dec 975 –84

Beaumont, Caitriona (2000) 'Citizens not Feminists: the boundary negotiated between citizenship and feminism by mainstream women's organisations in England' *Women's History Review* 9, 2, 411–426

Cahill, M and Jowitt, Tony (1977) 'The New Philanthropy: The Emergence of the Bradford City Guild of Help' *Jnl Soc Pol.,*9, 3, 359–82

Child, P (2019) 'Blacktown, Mass-Observation, and the dynamics of *voluntary action* in mid-twentieth-century England' *The Historical Journal* Open Access article

Coats, A W (1961) 'American Scholarship comes of Age: the Louisiana Purchase Exposition, 1904' *Jnl of the History of Ideas,* 22, 3, 404–417

Dresser, Madge (1984) 'Housing Policy in Bristol 1919–30' in M J Daunton *Councillors and Tenants: Local Authority housing in English cities 1919–1930* Leicester, Leicester University Press

Finlayson Geoffrey (1990) 'A Moving Frontier: Voluntarism and the State in British Social Welfare 1911–1949' *Twentieth Century British History,* 1,2,199

Hannam, June 'An enlarged sphere of usefulness: the Bristol Women's Movement c1860–1914' 184–209 in M Dresser and P Ollerenshaw (eds) (1996) *The Making of Modern Bristol* Tiverton, Redcliffe Press

Harris, José (2011) 'Voluntarism, the state and public-private partnerships in Beveridge's social thought' in M Oppenheimer and N Deakin (eds) *Beveridge and Voluntary Action in Britain and the Wider British World* Manchester, Manchester University Press

Harrison, M (1985) 'Art and Philanthropy: T C Horsfall and the Manchester Art Museum' in Alan J Kidd and K W Roberts *City, Class and Culture: studies of cultural production and social policy in Victorian Manchester* Manchester, Manchester University Press

Lewis, Jane (1996) 'The Boundary between voluntary and statutory social service in the late nineteenth and early twentieth centuries' *The Historical Journal,* 39, 1, 155–177

Martin, Moira (2008) 'Single Women and Philanthropy: a case study of women's associational life in Bristol 1880–1914' *Women's History Review, July,* 17,3, 395–417

Matthew-Jones, Lucinda (2016) 'I still remain one of the old Settlement boys': cross-class friendship in the First World War Letters of Cardiff University Settlement Lads' Club' *Cultural and Social History,* 13, 2, 195–21

Moore, Michael J (1977) 'Social Work and Social Welfare: the Organization of Philanthropic Resources in Britain 1900–1914' *Journal of British Studies,* 16, 2, 85–104

Reinders, Robert C (1982) 'Toynbee Hall and the American Settlement' *Social Service Review* 56, 1, 39–54

Oxford Dictionary of National Biography

Goldman, Lawrence (2004) 'Tawney, Richard Henry (1880–1962) historian and political thinker'

Hannam, June (2004) 'Gregory, Alice Sophia (1867–1946) midwife'

Holton, Sandra Stanley (2016) 'Hilda Clark (1881–1955) physician and war relief worker'

Pederson, Susan (2004) 'Macadam, Elizabeth (1871–1948) social worker' Philpot, Terry (2013) 'Simey [née Todd] Margaret Bayne, Lady Simey 1906–2004.

Simey, Margaret (2004) 'D'Aeth, Frederic George (1875–1940) social administrator and lecturer in social work'.

Sadler, John (2004) 'Percival, John (1834–1918)'.

Thomas, John B (2004) 'Pease, Marian Fry (1859–1943) education lecturer, administrator and social worker'.

Thomas, John B (2004) 'Cashmore, Hilda (1876–1943) university teacher and welfare worker'.

Williamson, Philip (2004) 'Bondfield, Margaret Grace (1873–1953) trade unionist, campaigner for women's interests and politician'.

Theses and web pages

Jennifer Rosemary Harrow 'The Development of University Settlements in England 1884–1939', unpublished PhD thesis, London School of Economics and Political Science, 1987

Alice Southern 'The Rowntree History Series and the Growth of Liberal Quakerism 1895–1925', unpublished M.Phil, University of Birmingham, 2010

Claire Davey 'Teacher Training in Bristol 1892–1930: a comparison across gender and through time', Prize Undergraduate Dissertation, University of Bristol, 2012

http://infed.org/ 'Mary Parker Follett, community, creative experience and education' with a list of her publications

Illustrations

Page iv Hilda Cashmore—M Pease (ed) *Hilda Cashmore 1876–1943* (1944) Printed for private circulation by John Bellows Ltd Gloucester.

Page viii Marian Pease—*The Magazine of the University Settlement Bristol*, Autumn 1950, no. 5 BRL B23991. Bristol Central Reference Library.

Page viii University College—Samuel Loxton (1857–1922). Bristol Central Reference Library.

Page 7 Toynbee Hall—H Barnett (1921 edit) *Canon Barnett: his life, work and friends, by his wife* London, John Murray.

Page 7 Whitechaple Gallery—H Barnett (1921 edit) *Canon Barnett: his life, work and friends, by his wife* London, John Murray.

Page 11 Professor Conwy Lloyd Morgan—*The Bristol University College Gazette.* Vol 1, February 2908–October 1909, Bristol, J W Arrowsmith.

Page 11 George Hare Leonard—Bristol Local History Collection, Bristol Central Reference Library.

Page 12 Heulwen Isambard Owen (1963)—*Sir Isambard Owen: a Biography* Caernarvon, Gwenlyn Evans.

Page 14 University Settlement—Samuel Loxton (1857–1922). Bristol Central Reference Library.

Page 17 Rev. S. A. and Mrs Barnett—H Barnett (1921 edit) *Canon Barnett: his life, work and friends, by his wife* London, John Murray.

Page 29 Great Western Cotton Works—Samuel Loxton (1857–1922). Bristol Central Reference Library.

Page 29 Cotton workers—Samuel Loxton (1857–1922). Bristol Central Reference Library.

Page 30 Margaret Bondfield—Harris & Ewing, 1922. Library of Congress, Washington D.C.

Page 33 Mothers and babies—Jennings Hilda (1971) *Sixty Years of Change: the Bristol University Settlement 1911-1971* Bristol, University Settlement Bristol Community Association.

Page 51 Whitsun Festival—https://www.bartonhillsettlement.org.uk/wp-content/uploads/2018/11/Barton-Hill-Settlement-History.pdf

Page 55 Ebenezer Howard diagram—Ebenezer Howard (1898) *TOMORROW: a peaceful path to real reform* London, Swan Sonnenschein and Co. Ltd.

Page 62 Bristol Women's Co-operative Guild—Edward Jackson (1911) *A Study in Democracy - being an account of the rise and progress of industrial co-operation in Bristol* Manchester Co-operative Wholesale Society's Printing Works.

Page 69 COS diagram—Redrawn from Michael Cahill and Tony Jowett (1977) 'The New Philanthropy: the emergence of the Bradford City Guild of Help' *Jnl Social Policy* 9,3, 380.

Page 69 Cashmore's diagram—Redrawn from Hilda Cashmore (1926) 'Settlements and Citizenship' A/TOY/022/022/044 London Metropolitan Archives.

Page 75 Football team—https://www.bartonhillsettlement.org.uk/wp-content/uploads/2018/11/Barton-Hill-Settlement-History.pdf.

Page 76 Sir Wyndham Deedes—Margaret Brasnett (1969) *Voluntary Social Action: a history of The National Council of Social Service* NCSS, 26 Bedford Square

London WC1.

Page 94 Jamai Ashram—M Pease (ed) *Hilda Cashmore 1876–1943* (1944) Printed for private circulation by John Bellows Ltd Gloucester.

Page 106 Bristol University Settlement—Bristol Local History Collection, Bristol Central Reference Library.

Page 106 Rag Week—J G Macqueen and SW Taylor (eds) (1976) *University and Community. Essays to mark the centenary of the founding of Bristol University College Bristol*, University of Bristol.

Page 113 Young and old—J G Macqueen and SW Taylor (eds) (1976) *University and Community. Essays to mark the centenary of the founding of Bristol University College Bristol*, University of Bristol.

Acknowledgements

This pamphlet started life as a lecture for the 50th Centenary of the Joseph Bettey Lecture at the Bristol and Avon Local History Association. I am most grateful to Peter Malpass for originally inviting me to give it. The Radical History Group then asked me to develop it into a study of Hilda Cashmore. My thanks to Trish Mensah and Barbara Segal who have read the text with great care and asked many helpful questions. I'm also very grateful to Richard Musgrove of the Bristol Radical History Group for his patience, tact and expertise in getting the manuscript through the press. My biggest debt is to Dawn Dyer, Librarian of the Local History Collection at the Bristol Central Library who guided me to sources and found illustrations for me since I could only make a couple of brief visits to Bristol during the time I've been engaged on the manuscript. Graham Tratt at the Bristol Archives, MR Dicomites at the Special Collections Women's Archive, London School of Economics and Helen Fisher at the Cadbury Research Library: Special Collections, University of Birmingham have all been particularly helpful. Also, thanks to Matt Davies of the University of Nottingham Humanities Digital Hub who worked to make poor quality images better for publication.

Special thanks too, to friends from the University of the West of England and the Regional History Centre, especially Madge Dresser, who sent me her thesis on Bristol housing and Moira Martin, whose work on Bristol women has informed my own. A very special thanks to June Hannam, who read two earlier drafts, offered very helpful comments and shared her encyclopaedic knowledge of women's history and Bristol so generously. I'm also most grateful to two friends and scholars, Jean Birrell in Birmingham and Elizabeth Boa in Nottingham, who read numerous drafts and did preliminary copy editing of the final text.